THE JOYS OF VEGETARIAN COOKING

The Joys of Vegetarian Cooking

OVER 200 DELICIOUS RECIPES
PRACTICAL, QUICK AND EASY

TARLA DALAL

VAKILS, FEFFER AND SIMONS LIMITED
Hague Building, 9, Sprott Road, Ballard Estate
Bombay 400 038

First printing: 1983

Second printing: 1984

By the same author

The Pleasures of Vegetarian Cooking

The Delights of Vegetarian Cooking

Atithya (Hindi)

Aaswadan (Hindi)

Price: Rs. 78/-

Published by Mrs. A. F. Shaikh for Vakils, Feffer and Simons Ltd.
Hague Building, 9, Sprott Road, Ballard Estate, Bombay 400 038

Printed by Arun K. Mehta at Vakil & Sons Ltd.,
Vakils House, Sprott Road, 18 Ballard Estate, Bombay 400 038

Designed by Vakils Art Department
Photographs by D. F. Poonawala
Cover and Page No. 63 Photographs by Ram Prabhu

CONTENTS

INTRODUCTION

This book is a sequel to THE PLEASURES OF VEGETARIAN COOKING and THE DELIGHTS OF VEGETARIAN COOKING. The emphasis, as in my earlier books, is on simple, quick and relatively economical dishes. To make it easier for beginners and to facilitate reproducibility, the procedures are given stepwise in simple language and using a minimum of technical culinary terms. As usual, with a view to making the book self-contained, all the basic recipes referred to in individual recipes are reproduced in the last section by way of ready reference.

The arrangement of this book follows, with some modifications, that used in the earlier books. And a new section on Dieters' Menu has been added in response to numerous personal requests. Another new section which is not only interesting but also very colourful pertains to Tabletop Cookery. Many hostesses are reluctant to cook in front of guests and this is understandable because it usually requires very careful advance preparation. However, if you follow the recipes and instructions with care, I assure you that you will not find such cooking difficult. What is more, you will discover that it is a sure way to enliven a party and often, as for flambé desserts, also an impressive way. Only take care not to try out more than one tabletop dish at a party until such time as you have gained sufficient practice and confidence with each separate dish.

For those of you who are not familiar with my earlier books, may I request that you read the various introductory notes before trying out any recipe. I do hope that this book will give you and your family members many moments of joy and happiness.

— Tarla Dalal

WEIGHTS, MEASURES, TEMPERATURES AND TIMES

Weights

Weights are given in grams or kilograms (kg.) with the corresponding figure of ounces (oz.) or pounds (lb.) indicated in brackets.

In the bulk of the recipes, the weight in grams is rounded off to the nearest multiple of 25 grams for convenience and ease in weighing. Where, however, weighing must necessarily be done accurately, e.g., for cakes, pastries, biscuits, icings, etc., the rounding off to grams has been done to the nearest multiple of 5 grams according to the following conversion table:

Oz.	Exact conversion in grams (rounded off)	Corresponding grams rounded off to multiple of 5 as given in the recipes
½	14	15
1	28	25
1½	42	40
1¾	50	50
2	57	55
2½	71	70
3	85	85
3½	99	100
4	113	115
4½	127	125
5	142	140
6	170	170
7	198	200
8	227	225
9	255	255
10	284	285
10½	298	300
11	312	310
12	340	340

For ingredients available in cans or packets, the net weights of the ingredients in grams have been indicated in brackets as a guide. In most cases, it will not matter if a can or packet of slightly different weight is used. The exceptions are condensed milk and gelatine; and in the latter case, the use of a strong gelatine (e.g., of any standard international make) is recommended.

Measures

Where actual volumetric measurement has to be done, the measures are given in millilitres (ml.) or litres with the corresponding figure of Imperial fluid ounces (fl. oz.) or pints in brackets. The approximate conversion rate of 30 ml. = 1 fl. oz. has been used.

Other measures used are

teacup   measure full to the brim. The average Indian teacup is about 210 ml. (7 fl. oz.) and corresponding adjustments should be made if using larger size teacups.

teaspoon	for liquids, measure full to the brim. For solids, use a heaped spoon unless the recipe specifically states level spoon. The volumetric content is about 5 ml. ($\frac{1}{6}$ fl. oz.)
tablespoon	measure as for teaspoon. The volumetric content is about 15 ml. ($\frac{1}{2}$ fl. oz.) or approximately equal to 3 teaspoons.

Temperatures

The recipes state whether the oven should be slow, moderate, hot or very hot and give the indicative temperature in degrees Fahrenheit as a guide. The actual instructions of the oven manufacturer should be referred to for further guidance and adjustments made according to experience and results, where necessary.

The following conversion chart will prove of assistance:

Oven	°F	°C	Gas Mark
Slow	250-300	121-149	$\frac{1}{2}$, 1, 2
Moderate	325-375	163-190	3, 4
Hot	400-450	204-233	5, 6, 7
Very hot	475-500	246-260	8, 9

Times

The preparation and cooking times stated against individual recipes are merely indicative and are given purely by way of guidance for meal planning. Actual timings will certainly vary from individual to individual. The time for cutting vegetables, etc., is included in the preparation time but the times for soaking, freezing, etc., as also the times for preparing ingredients in the form of recipes (e.g., cake mixture, pastry, etc.) have not been included.

NOTES ON INGREDIENTS

Most of the ingredients required for use in the recipes are easily available in India although in places other than the metropolitan cities, there may be occasional difficulty in procuring a few items which are not in common use.

The following will, however, serve as a general guide and also enable substitution of certain items outside India.

1. **Cheeses:**

(a) **Paneer:** This is a dry form of cottage cheese readily available in India. If not available, you can first make chhanna as under and thereafter can press the chhanna into a rectangular shape and squeeze out the water to obtain paneer.

Boil 1 litre (1¾ pints) of milk while stirring continuously, add the juice of 1 lemon (or alternatively 1 teacup of curds and ½ teaspoon of salt) and stir gently till all the milk curdles. Leave covered for some time and strain through a muslin cloth. The moist solid left in the cloth is chhanna — which is in-between cottage cheese and soft cream cheese.

(b) **Cooking Cheese:** Use the variety which is termed cooking cheese and which melts readily while cooking.

(c) **General:** Where the recipe states just "cheese" or "table cheese," you can use any processed cheese.

2. **Curds:** Yoghurt can be used as a substitute.

3. **Fats:** The fats specified in the recipes are all vegetarian. Butter and margarine are entirely interchangeable although in certain cases (e.g. cakes), butter does give better results.

As regards ghee, hydrogenated oils (e.g. Vanaspati type ghee) can also be used instead. Butter cannot always be used in place of ghee in many Indian dishes, e.g., parathas, Indian sweets etc. You can however make ghee at home from butter by boiling butter in a pan until the ghee separates and floats clear on top. The floating ghee should be strained and stored for use as it keeps for long periods without spoiling.

4. **Oils:** The ordinary oil referred to in the recipes is refined groundnut or refined sesame ("til") oil. If this is not available, you can use salad oil or any cooking oil but each oil will impart its own characteristic flavour to the preparation.

5. **Flours:** The flours referred in the recipes are:

bajra flour	flour made from bajra
cornflour	readymade flour sold by that name
gram flour	besan or flour made from grams
maize flour	makai-ka-atta or flour made from maize

plain flour	maida
rice flour	chawal-ka-atta or flour made from rice
self-raising flour	flour containing baking powder
whole meal flour	gehun-ka-atta or flour made from wheat

6. **Khoya:** This is also called "mawa" and is readily available in India. It is made by boiling milk in a broad vessel and stirring continuously until a thick residue is left.

7. **Masalas:** For best results, dry masala powders should be freshly ground. A few special masala powders have been given in individual recipes. A very commonly used masala is garam masala which is usually available in the market in ready-made form. It is a powdered mixture of black pepper, cloves and other spices such as cinnamon.

Names of Ingredients: By and large, the English names of ingredients have been used and in a few cases, the Hindi names. Care has been taken to avoid the use of more than one name for any given ingredient.

Selective Glossary of Hindi and English Names

ajinomoto powder	a popular brand name for mono sodium glutamate (you can use any other make)
ajwain	a type of spice like thymol seeds
amchur powder	dried mango powder
aniseed	saunf
bay leaves	tej patta
besan	gram flour
besan bundi	small fried crisp savoury drops made from gram flour
channa	gram
curry leaves	sweet neem leaves
dhana-jira powder	coriander-cumin seed powder
fenugreek	methi
jaggery (gur)	a sweet product made from sugarcane
khus-khus	poppy seeds
makhana	lotus seeds
math	a brown coloured lentil, also known as matki
nutmeg	jaiphal
palak	spinach
pumpkin, red	kaddu, kohlu
pumpkin, white	lauki, dudhi
rajma	a variety of kidney beans
ridge gourd	torai, turiya
sesame	til
sev	vermicelli type of preparation made from gram flour
shah-jira	black cumin seed
salt, black	a type of rock salt known locally as kala namak, sanchal
tondli	a vegetable of the size of gherkins, also known as tendli, tindola

TERMS USED IN COOKING

appetiser	a small tasty portion of food or a drink served before dinner.
bake	to cook by dry heat in oven.
baking blind	the method of baking flans, tarts and other pastry cases without a filling.
batter	any mixture of dry ingredients and liquid that is stirred or beaten and can be poured.
beat	to introduce air into a mixture by a vigorous over and over motion, using a wooden spoon, wire whisk, fork or electric beater.
bind	to add a liquid, egg or melted fat to a dry mixture to hold it together.
blanch	to put food in boiling water in order to either whiten or remove the skin.
blend	to combine all ingredients thoroughly until very smooth and uniform.
boil	to cook at boiling point.
brown	to put a cooked dish or meringue under grill or in the oven for a short time to give a golden colour.
brush	to spread thinly with a brush.
canapé	an appetiser of seasoned food usually served on little pieces of crisp toast or crackers.
casserole	a baking dish usually oven-proof with a tight-fitting lid. Food cooked in a casserole is served straight from it.
chop	to cut food into very small pieces with a sharp knife.
chafing dish	a dish for cooking on the table.
coat	to cover food with a thin layer of flour, egg, bread crumbs or batter.
colander	a vessel having small holes in the bottom, used as a strainer.
consistency	a term describing the texture, usually the thickness of a mixture.
cream	to beat fat and sugar to incorporate air, break down the sugar crystals and soften the fat. This can be done either by rubbing or working ingredients against the side of the bowl with a wooden spoon or fork.
core	to remove inner portion.

croutons	small cubes of bread, fried or toasted until crisp.
cubes	small equal pieces, usually of about 12 mm. (½″) each side.
deep fry	to cook a food in a deep layer of hot fat.
dice	to cut into small cubes, generally of about 6 mm. (¼″) size.
dissolve	to make a solution with a liquid and a dry substance e.g. sugar and water.
dot	to scatter small amounts of butter, nuts, chocolate etc. over the surface of a food.
dough	a mixture of flour and liquid in combination with other ingredients, thick enough to knead and roll.
dredge	to coat food with some ingredients such as seasoned flour or sugar.
dust	to sprinkle or coat lightly with flour or sugar.
fat	a term used for butter, margarine, ghee and hydrogenated oils (like vanaspati).
flambé	to cover a food with brandy etc., then light and serve flaming.
fold in	to combine two mixtures (e.g. adding beaten egg-whites to a soufflé) very gently with a wire whisk or spoon using an under-and-over motion, until thoroughly mixed.
fry	to cook in a small amount of fat.
garnish	to decorate with portions of colourful and contrasting food.
glacé	coated with a thin sugar syrup cooked to the crack stage e.g. glacé cherries.
glaze	to add lustre or shine to a food by coating with syrup or jelly.
grate	to shred foods by rubbing against a grater.
grill	to cook directly under a flame or heating in an oven.
grind	to cut or crush ingredients into powder form.
herbs	aromatic plants used for garnishing and seasoning.
icing	the process of covering with a sugar coating; or the coating itself.
knead	to work and press the dough hard with the heels of the hands so that the dough becomes stretched and elastic.
marinate	to soak food in liquid (e.g. lemon juice or a mixture such as french dressing) that will flavour it.
meringue	stiffly beaten mixture of egg-whites and sugar used to cover the top of a pie and browned in the oven or made into small cakes or cookies and baked.
melt	to heat solid ingredients until they become liquid.
mix	to stir, usually with a spoon, until the ingredients are thoroughly combined.
pare	to cut off the outside skin with a knife e.g. from potatoes or apples.
peel	to strip off the outer covering e.g. for oranges.

15

pit	to remove seeds from fruit.
prove	to allow the dough to rise until it has increased its bulk to twice the original size, by putting it in a warm place.
purée	a smooth thick mixture obtained by passing cooked food through a sieve (do not confuse with the Hindi term "puri").
pre-heat	to heat oven to stated temperature before product goes in.
sauté	to fry foods in a small amount of fat until golden and tender.
scoop	to remove the inner portion and make hollow with a scoop-shaped spoon.
sift	to pass through a fine sieve so as to remove lumps.
simmer	to boil on a slow flame.
skewer	a long pin, usually of metal, used for cooking a number of food pieces at the same time.
slivers	long thin pieces (usually almonds).
soak	to immerse in liquid for a time.
soufflé	a light dish incorporating a lot of air. It can either be a hot baked dish or a cold one.
steam	to cook in the steam which arises from a pan of boiling water.
stew	to cook slowly in a small amount of liquid for a long time.
stir	to mix with a spoon etc., using a rotary motion.
stock	the liquid in which vegetables are cooked.
stone	to remove seed from fruit.
strain	to filter coarsely, to remove food from liquid.
toast	to brown and dry the surface of foods such as bread or nuts by heating.
toss	to lightly mix ingredients without mashing them e.g. for salads.
until set	until the liquid has become firm—often refers to a gelatine, jelly or custard mixture.
whip	to beat rapidly to produce expansion through the incorporation of air, as in egg-whites and whipped cream.

I. Drinks

ORANGE AND LEMON DRINK PICTURE ON PAGE 45

A drink which makes your guest feel very special.
Preparation time: a few minutes · No cooking · Makes 1 large glass.

1 bottle Limca
1 tablespoon vanilla ice-cream
1 teaspoon lemon juice
1 tablespoon orange squash
crushed ice and chopped fruit to
   serve

1. Blend the Limca, ice-cream, lemon juice and orange squash in a liquidiser.
2. Top with crushed ice and chopped fruit.

★ Serve cold.

GINGER-ALE FUZZ

A colourful drink with the taste of ginger.
Preparation time: a few minutes · No cooking · Makes 1 large glass.

1 tablespoon vanilla ice-cream
¾ bottle ginger-ale
1 teaspoon orange squash

1. Chill the ginger-ale.
2. Put the ice-cream and orange squash in a tall glass.
3. Pour the chilled ginger-ale on top.

★ Serve immediately.

FRUIT PUNCH

A delightful combination of fruit juices and milk.
Preparation time: a few minutes · No cooking · Makes 1 large glass.

80 ml. (2⅔ fl. oz.) pineapple juice
40 ml. (1⅓ fl. oz.) mango juice
40 ml. (1⅓ fl. oz.) orange juice
15 ml. (½ fl. oz.) pomegranate
   syrup
60 ml. (2 fl. oz.) milk
crushed ice to serve

Mix all the ingredients and fill balance glass with crushed ice.

★ Serve immediately.

17

FRUIT CUP

Light and colourful.
Preparation time: a few minutes · No cooking · Makes 1 large glass.

1 tablespoon pomegranate
  syrup
1½ teaspoons orange squash
½ teaspoon lemon squash *or*
  juice of lime
2 tablespoons chopped fruit
  (oranges, pineapple, apples,
  bananas)
¼ bottle lemonade
¼ bottle soda
lemon slice for decoration
crushed ice to serve

Mix the ingredients and pour into a tall glass. Add lots of crushed ice, decorate with a lemon slice.

★ Serve with a tall spoon.

PINA COLADA PICTURE ON PAGE 25

An exotic golden drink from the land of palm trees.
Preparation time: a few minutes · No cooking · Makes 6 glasses.

1 large can (850 grams)
  pineapple juice
5 tablespoons pineapple syrup
2 large fresh coconuts
1 family pack (½ litre) vanilla
  ice-cream
3 tablespoons powdered sugar

1. Grate the coconuts. Add 6 teacups of water and allow to stand for a little while. Blend in a liquidiser and strain.
2. Add the sugar and put to chill.
3. Blend the pineapple juice, pineapple syrup, vanilla ice-cream and the chilled coconut milk in a liquidiser.

★ Serve cold.

Note: If fresh coconuts are not available, you can use frozen coconut meat. But in any event, do not use desiccated coconut.

II. Cocktail Snacks

CHINESE STYLE SAMOSAS PICTURE ON PAGE 25

Small and dainty samosas served with garlic flavoured tomato sauce.
Preparation time: 15 to 20 minutes · Cooking time: 15 minutes · Makes 15 to 20 samosas.

For the stuffing
1 teacup boiled noodles
2 teacups shredded cabbage
2 sliced onions
1 grated carrot
1 teacup bean sprouts
1 teaspoon soya sauce
½ teaspoon Ajinomoto powder
2 tablespoons oil
salt to taste
oil for deep frying

For the dough
1½ teacups plain flour
½ teaspoon salt
3 teaspoons oil

For the spicy tomato sauce
1 teacup tomato ketchup
a small piece ginger
4 cloves garlic
2 teaspoons chilli sauce
¼ teaspoon salt

For the stuffing
1. Heat the oil on a high flame.
2. Add the cabbage, onions, carrot, bean sprouts and Ajinomoto powder and cook for 3 minutes.
3. Add the noodles, soya sauce and salt.

For the dough
1. Mix all the ingredients and add water to make a stiff dough.
2. Roll out into very thin circles.

For the spicy tomato sauce
1. Grind the ginger and garlic into a paste.
2. Mix the paste with the remaining ingredients.

How to proceed
1. Put a little stuffing on each circle and fold over to form a semi-circle. Bring the ends together and press. Repeat for the remaining circles.
2. Deep fry in oil until crisp.

★ Serve with spicy tomato sauce.

19

SUN KABABS

A tasty snack.
Preparation time: 15 minutes · Cooking time: 10 to 15 minutes · Makes 30 to 40 small kababs.

1 teacup grated cauliflower
1 teacup grated cabbage
1 boiled and mashed potato
1 teacup grated paneer
1 tablespoon chopped coriander
3 to 4 chopped green chillies
1 teaspoon cumin seeds
2 pinches Ajinomoto powder
1 tablespoon ghee
salt to taste

For frying
1 teacup gram flour
1½ teacups water
½ teaspoon chilli powder
½ teaspoon salt
oil for deep frying

1. Heat the ghee and fry the cumin seeds.
2. Add the raw cauliflower and cabbage and the Ajinomoto powder and cook for a few minutes.
3. Add the potato, paneer, coriander, green chillies and salt.
4. Cool the mixture and then shape into rounds. Flatten the rounds.
5. Make a batter by mixing the gram flour, water, chilli powder and salt. Dip the kababs in this batter and deep fry in oil.

★ Serve hot.

HOT CHEESE SQUARES

A popular snack.
Preparation time: 15 minutes · Cooking time: 10 minutes · Makes 20 to 25 pieces.

3 tablespoons grated cheese
3 tablespoons soft butter
1 teaspoon vinegar
½ teaspoon baking powder
1 level teaspoon mustard powder
3 tablespoons gram flour
3 to 4 chopped green chillies
1 to 2 teaspoons milk
5 to 6 lightly toasted bread slices
very little salt

1. Beat the cheese and butter very well.
2. Add the vinegar, baking powder, mustard powder and beat again.
3. Add the gram flour, chillies, milk and very little salt.
4. Apply the mixture thickly on the bread slices.
5. Bake in a hot oven at 450°F for 10 minutes. Alternatively, grill for a few minutes.

★ Cut into small squares and serve hot.

CORN AND PANEER CANAPÉS

Tender corn and paneer make an excellent canapé combination.
Preparation time: 10 minutes · Cooking time: 15 minutes · Makes about 40 canapés.

For the base
10 bread slices
a little butter

For the spread
2 teacups white sauce, *page 164*
1½ teacups cooked corn *or* frozen corn
1 teacup chopped paneer
2 tablespoons chopped coriander
3 chopped green chillies
2 pinches sugar
4 tablespoons grated cooking cheese
salt and pepper to taste
chilli sauce to serve

1. Cut the bread slices into small rounds. Apply a little butter on both sides and bake in a hot oven at 400°F for 5 to 10 minutes until crisp.
2. Mix the corn, paneer, white sauce, coriander, green chillies, sugar, salt and pepper.
3. Spread a little corn mixture on each toasted round. Sprinkle grated cheese on top and bake in a hot oven at 400°F until the cheese melts.

★ Dot with chilli sauce and serve hot.

CHEESE TOPPED CREAM CRACKERS
PICTURE ON PAGE 25

A spicy version of cheese on biscuits.
Preparation time: 5 minutes · Cooking time: 10 minutes · Makes 16 pieces.

8 cream cracker biscuits
2 tablespoons soft butter
5 tablespoons grated table cheese
1 tablespoon grated cooking cheese
1 teaspoon plain flour
1 teaspoon milk
2 pinches baking powder
2 pinches salt
2 pinches chilli powder (optional)

1. Mix the butter, table cheese, flour, milk, baking powder, salt and chilli powder.
2. Spread thickly on the biscuits.
3. Sprinkle a little grated cooking cheese.
4. Grill for 3 to 4 minutes or bake in a hot oven at 400°F for 10 minutes.

★ Cut into triangles and serve hot.

CHEESE TRIANGLES

Something different-looking with cheese.
Preparation time: 10 minutes · Cooking time: 15 minutes · Makes 25 to 30 pieces.

a few large slices fresh bread
2 tablespoons soft butter
½ teaspoon mustard powder
1 teacup white sauce, *page 164*
4 tablespoons grated cooking
   cheese
salt and pepper to taste

1. Remove the crust and cut each bread slice into four.
2. Thin the bread slices by rolling out.
3. Mix the butter and mustard powder and apply this mixture on the bread pieces.
4. Make triangles by holding two opposite corners of each bread piece and by fastening with toothpicks.
5. Arrange the triangles on a baking tin and bake in a hot oven at 450°F for 5 to 7 minutes until crisp.
6. Add salt, pepper and half of the cheese to the white sauce.
7. When you wish to serve, fill a little seasoned white sauce in the fold of each triangle. Top with the remaining cheese and bake in a hot oven at 450°F for 5 minutes.

★ Serve hot.

CHEESY PUFFS PICTURE ON PAGE 25

Hot, crisp and cheesy.
Preparation time: 5 minutes · Cooking time: 10 minutes · Makes 24 pieces.

12 khari biscuits *or* golden puffs
1½ teacups white sauce,
   page 164
1 chopped green chilli (optional)
4 tablespoons grated cooking
   cheese
a little chilli powder
salt and pepper to taste

1. Mix the white sauce, green chilli, half the cheese, salt and pepper.
2. Divide each biscuit into 2 parts.
3. Arrange on a baking tray.
4. On each biscuit, spread a little sauce, sprinkle some cheese and chilli powder.
5. Bake in a hot oven at 450°F for 2 to 3 minutes or grill for a few minutes.

   ★ Serve hot.

CHEESE AND CARROT ROLLS PICTURE ON PAGE 25

Unusually tasty.
Preparation time: 15 minutes · Cooking time: 15 minutes · Makes approximately 25 rolls.

3 to 4 grated carrots
3 tablespoons grated cheese
3 tablespoons butter
2 chopped green chillies
1 teaspoon white vinegar
1 level teaspoon mustard
   powder
a few slices fresh bread
salt to taste
melted butter

1. Remove the crust from the bread slices. Roll out the slices and keep in a wet napkin.
2. Mix the carrots, cheese, butter, chillies, mustard powder, vinegar and salt.
3. Spread a little of this mixture on each bread slice. Roll up each slice tightly.
4. Cut each roll into 3 parts. Fasten each roll with a toothpick.
5. Arrange on a greased baking tray and apply a little melted butter on top of each roll.
6. Bake in a hot oven at 400°F for 10 to 15 minutes.

   ★ Serve hot.

SPINACH WAFFLES PICTURE ON FACING PAGE

An unusual savoury waffle.
Preparation time: a few minutes · Cooking time: a few minutes · Makes 6 to 8 pieces.

2 teacups gram flour
1½ teacups chopped spinach
4 to 5 ground green chillies
¼ teaspoon asafoetida
1 tablespoon oil
½ teaspoon soda bi-carb
green chutney to serve

1. Mix all the ingredients and add enough water to make a thick batter.
2. Pour a little batter at a time into a heated and well-greased waffle iron and cook at a moderate temperature till crisp.

★ Serve hot with green chutney.

Note: You can also use fenugreek leaves (methi bhaji) instead of spinach.

SPINACH CANAPÉS PICTURE ON FACING PAGE

Colourful and tasty.
Preparation time: 10 minutes · Cooking time: 15 minutes · Makes about 40 canapés.

For the base
10 bread slices
a little butter

For the spread
3 teacups chopped spinach
1 chopped onion
2 to 3 chopped green chillies
a pinch soda bi-carb
2 tablespoons chopped paneer
4 tablespoons grated cooking cheese
2 tablespoons ghee
salt to taste

1. Cut the bread slices into small squares or rounds. Apply a little butter on both sides and bake in a hot oven at 400°F for 5 to 10 minutes until crisp.
2. Heat the ghee and fry the onion. Add the spinach, green chillies, soda bi-carb and salt. Cook for 3 to 4 minutes.
3. Add the chopped paneer and remove from the fire.
4. Spread a little spinach mixture on each toasted piece. Sprinkle grated cheese on top and bake in a hot oven at 400°F until the cheese melts.

★ Serve hot.

FACING PAGE
1 SPINACH CANAPÉS
2 CHEESE TOPPED CREAM CRACKERS
3 CHEESY PUFFS
4 SPINACH WAFFLES
5 MUSHROOM AND ONION FONDUE
6 PINA COLADA
7 CHINESE STYLE SAMOSAS
8 CHEESE AND CARROT ROLLS

CREAM OF MUSHROOM SOUP PICTURE ON FACING PAGE

A delicately flavoured soup.
Preparation time: 10 minutes · Cooking time: 25 minutes · Serves 6.

250 grams (9 oz.) fresh
   mushrooms
2 onions
1 potato
100 grams (4 oz.) fresh cream
2 tablespoons butter
salt and pepper to taste
chopped parsley for decoration
   (optional)

1. Chop the mushrooms, onions and potato.
2. Heat the butter and fry the onions and mushrooms for at least 5 to 6 minutes. Take out and keep aside a little of the mushrooms and onion mixture.
3. Add the potatoes and fry again for 3 to 4 minutes.
4. Add 6 teacups of water and cook in a pressure cooker.
5. When cooked, blend in a liquidiser and strain.
6. Add the balance mushrooms and onion mixture to the soup and boil for 10 minutes.
7. Add salt, pepper and the cream.

★ Serve hot garnished with chopped parsley.

FACING PAGE
1 NOODLES WITH TOMATO AND CREAM SAUCES
2 CREAM OF MUSHROOM SOUP

27

FRUIT AND NUT SOUP

A delicately flavoured soup.
Preparation time: 15 minutes · Cooking time: 20 minutes · Serves 6 to 8.

2 sliced potatoes
1 chopped onion
4 chopped spring onions with leaves
4 to 5 sticks celery, chopped
200 grams (7 oz.) fresh cream
1 tablespoon butter
salt and pepper to taste
grated cheese, toasted almonds and grapes to serve

1. Heat the butter and fry the onions, spring onions and celery for at least 3 to 4 minutes.
2. Add the potatoes and fry again for a little while.
3. Add 5 teacups of water and cook.
4. When cooked, blend in a liquidiser and strain.
5. Boil the soup for a few minutes.
6. Beat the cream and add three-quarters to the soup.
7. Add salt and pepper and mix well.

★ Serve hot topped with the balance cream, grated cheese, almonds and grapes.

Variation 1: CREAM OF CELERY SOUP Add a few more sticks of celery and omit grated cheese, almonds and grapes.
Variation 2: CREAM OF ALMOND SOUP Put 20 almonds in the stock and omit cheese and grapes.

CREOLE SOUP

Easy to prepare and inexpensive.
Preparation time: 15 minutes · Cooking time: 30 minutes · Serves 6 to 8.

For the stock
3 onions
3 potatoes
3 tomatoes

For the topping
1 chopped onion
1 large capsicum, finely chopped
2 finely chopped tomatoes
2 tablespoons tomato ketchup
½ teaspoon paprika
2 tablespoons refined oil
salt and pepper to taste

For the stock
1. Cut all the vegetables into big pieces, add 6 teacups of water and cook in a pressure cooker.
2. When cooked, blend in a liquidiser. Strain.

How to proceed
1. Heat the oil and fry the onion for 1 minute.
2. Add the capsicum and tomatoes and fry again for 2 minutes.
3. Add the stock and boil for 10 minutes.
4. Add the tomato ketchup, salt and pepper. Sprinkle the paprika on top.

★ Serve hot.

ONION AND CAULIFLOWER SOUP

Prepare this soup when you are short of time.
Preparation time: 5 minutes · Cooking time: 15 minutes · Serves 6 to 8.

½ litre (⅞ pint) milk
15 grams (½ oz.) cornflour
1 finely chopped onion
50 grams (2 oz.) finely chopped
   cauliflower
10 button mushrooms, finely
   sliced (optional)
5 bay leaves
2 sticks cinnamon
10 peppercorns
¼ teaspoon Ajinomoto powder
½ teaspoon nutmeg powder
50 grams (2 oz.) butter
salt and pepper to taste
chopped parsley to serve

1. Heat the butter and fry the onion for 1 minute.
   Add the bay leaves, cinnamon and
   peppercorns and fry again for ½ minute.
2. Add the cauliflower and mushrooms and fry
   for 1 minute.
3. Add the cornflour and fry for ½ minute.
4. Add the milk and ½ litre (⅞ pint) of water.
5. Add the Ajinomoto and nutmeg powders,
   salt and pepper. Cook for a few minutes.

★ Sprinkle parsley on top and serve hot.

QUICK CORN SOUP

Surprise unexpected guests with this tasty soup.
Preparation time: 5 minutes · Cooking time: 15 minutes · Serves 6 to 8.

¾ teacup cooked tender corn
   (frozen)
1 finely chopped onion
3 teacups milk
3 teacups water
1½ tablespoons plain flour
1 tablespoon butter
salt and pepper to taste

1. Mix the milk, water and flour.
2. Heat the butter and fry the onion for at least
   2 minutes.
3. Add the flour mixture and the corn.
4. Boil for 10 minutes. Stir in between and check
   that the soup does not stick to the bottom of
   the vessel.
5. Add salt and pepper.

★ Serve hot.

WINTER SOUP WITH RICE AND CHEESE BALLS PICTURE ON PAGE 35

Delicious cheese balls add both appearance and taste to this rich and golden soup.
Preparation time: 15 minutes · Cooking time: 25 minutes · Serves 6 to 8.

2 onions
2 potatoes
4 carrots
200 grams (7 oz.) white
   pumpkin
½ teacup fresh cream
1 teacup milk
1 tablespoon butter
cheese balls (see below)
salt and pepper to taste
chopped parsley to serve

1. Cut the vegetables into big pieces.
2. Wash, add 7 teacups of water and put to cook in a pressure cooker.
3. Blend the mixture in a liquidiser and strain the soup.
4. Add the butter and boil for 10 minutes.
5. Warm the milk.
6. When you want to serve, add the warmed milk, cream, salt and pepper.
7. Add the cheese balls and decorate with chopped parsley.

   ★ Serve hot.

For the cheese balls
2 tablespoons cooked rice
2 tablespoons grated cheese
2 tablespoons chopped parsley
2 level tablespoons plain flour
2 pinches chilli powder
2 pinches salt
ghee *or* refined oil to fry

For the cheese balls
1. Mix all the ingredients.
2. Shape into small round balls.
3. Deep fry in ghee.

   ★ Serve hot with the soup.

ONE MEAL SOUP

Hearty and warming. An unusual combination of vegetables and lentils.
Preparation time: 15 minutes · Cooking time: 30 minutes · Serves 6 to 8.

For the stock
2 onions
2 potatoes
1 tablespoon moong dal
(without skin)

For the topping
1 chopped onion
1 tablespoon chopped french
beans
2 tablespoons chopped
cauliflower
1 chopped carrot
1 chopped tomato
2 tablespoons boiled spaghetti
1 tablespoon butter
salt and pepper to taste
grated cheese and bread
croutons to serve

For the stock
1. Cut the onions and potatoes into big pieces.
   Add the moong dal and 5 teacups of water and
   cook in a pressure cooker.
2. When cooked, pass through a sieve.

How to proceed
1. Heat the butter and fry the onions for at least
   2 minutes.
2. Add the french beans, cauliflower and carrot
   and fry again for 2 to 3 minutes.
3. Add ½ teacup of water and cook till the
   vegetables are soft.
4. Add the stock and boil for 10 minutes.
5. Add the tomato, spaghetti, salt and pepper and
   boil again for 5 minutes.

★ Serve hot with grated cheese and bread croutons.

SPICY BEAN AND TOMATO SOUP PICTURE ON PAGE 81

One of the most simple and economical soups. Warm and spicy, welcoming for the
family on a cold or rainy day.
Preparation time: 10 minutes · Cooking time: 20 minutes · Serves 6 to 8.

1 teacup cooked rajma *or*
kidney beans
1 kg. (2¼ lb.) tomatoes
2 finely chopped onions
3 cloves crushed garlic
a pinch oregano *or* ajwain
(optional)
4 tablespoons boiled macaroni
or noodles
½ teaspoon chilli powder
½ teaspoon sugar
2 tablespoons oil
salt and pepper to taste
grated cheese to serve

1. Chop the tomatoes.
2. Heat the oil and fry the onion and crushed
   garlic for 1 minute.
3. Add the tomatoes and cook for 1 minute.
4. Add 6 teacups of water and cook until the
   onions are soft.
5. Blend the mixture in a liquidiser. Strain.
6. Add the rajma, macaroni, chilli powder, sugar,
   oregano, salt and pepper.

★ Serve hot with grated cheese.

MILANAISE SOUP PICTURE ON PAGE 64

A vegetarian version of an Italian soup, flavoured with tulsi leaves.
Preparation time: 15 minutes · Cooking time: 30 minutes · Serves 6 to 8.

For the stock
3 onions
3 potatoes
3 tomatoes

For the topping
1 finely chopped onion
1 teacup finely chopped
cabbage
1 large chopped tomato
2 tablespoons boiled macaroni
1 small can (225 grams) baked
beans
1 tablespoon finely chopped
basil leaves *or* tulsi paan
2 tablespoons refined oil
salt and pepper to taste
grated cheese to serve

For the stock
1. Cut the vegetables into big pieces, add 7 teacups of water and put to cook in a pressure cooker.
2. When cooked, blend in a liquidiser. Strain.

How to proceed
1. Heat the oil and fry the onion for 1 minute.
2. Add the cabbage and fry again for a little while.
3. Add the stock and boil for 10 minutes.
4. Add the tomato, macaroni, baked beans, basil leaves, salt and pepper and boil for a few minutes.

★ Serve hot with grated cheese.

ONION AND PEA SOUP PICTURE ON PAGE 36

A pleasing combination of fresh greens.
Preparation time: 15 minutes · Cooking time: 30 minutes · Serves 6 to 8.

4 chopped spring onions *or*
leeks
2 teacups chopped spinach
1 head lettuce, chopped
1 tablespoon chopped mint
2 teacups green peas
2 teacups milk
2 pinches nutmeg
2 tablespoons butter
salt and pepper to taste
chopped parsley to serve

1. Heat the butter, add the spring onions, spinach, lettuce and mint and cook for a few minutes.
2. Add the green peas and 4 teacups of water and cook in a pressure cooker.
3. When cooked, blend in a liquidiser. Strain.
4. Add the milk, salt and pepper. Sprinkle the nutmeg and chopped parsley on top.

★ Serve hot.

CREAM OF VEGETABLE SOUP

Creamy and hearty.
Preparation time: 15 minutes · Cooking time: 30 minutes · Serves 6 to 8.

For the stock
3 onions
3 potatoes

For the topping
1 finely chopped onion
1 teacup mixed boiled
  vegetables (french beans,
  carrots, green peas)
1 tablespoon butter
2 tablespoons fresh cream
2 teacups white sauce, *page 164*
2 tablespoons grated cheese
salt and pepper to taste

For the stock
1. Cut the onions and potatoes into big pieces.
2. Add 6 to 7 teacups of water and put to cook in a pressure cooker.
3. When cooked, blend the vegetables in a liquidiser and strain.

How to proceed
1. Heat the butter in a vessel and fry the onion for 1 minute.
2. Add the stock and cook for 5 minutes.
3. Add the vegetables, cream, white sauce, cheese, salt and pepper and mix well.

★ Serve hot.

Note: You can prepare different types of vegetable soups by changing the vegetable for the topping e.g. instead of 1 teacup of mixed vegetables, use 1 teacup of canned mushrooms or asparagus and add the liquid from the can to the stock.

ORANGE CASTLES PICTURE ON FACING PAGE

An attractive addition to a summer buffet.
Preparation time: 15 minutes · Setting time: 30 minutes · Serves 8 to 10.

1 packet (100 grams) orange jelly
1 small can (450 grams) pineapple slices *or* orange segments
1 teacup boiled mixed vegetables (french beans, carrots, green peas)
½ teacup boiled spaghetti
½ teacup cooked rice
4 teaspoons sugar
½ teaspoon salt
salt and pepper to taste
radish roses, shredded cabbage and salad leaves for decoration
Thousand Island dressing, *page 165, or* green goddess dressing, *page 39,* to serve.

1. Dissolve the jelly in 3 teacups of boiling water. Cool a little and add 2 teaspoons of sugar and ½ teaspoon of salt.
2. Pour 1½ tablespoons of the jelly mixture in castle moulds. Put to set in the refrigerator.
3. Drain and chop the fruit.
4. Mix the vegetables, spaghetti, rice and fruit. Add 2 teaspoons of sugar. Add salt and pepper.
5. Put a little of this mixture in each mould and pour the remaining jelly on top in all the moulds.
6. Put to set in the refrigerator.
7. Just before serving, dip the moulds in hot water for a few seconds, loosen the sides and unmould on a plate. Decorate with radish roses, shredded cabbage and salad leaves.

★ Serve with Thousand Island dressing.

FRUITY FRENCH DRESSING

An unusual version of the famous dressing, good with fresh vegetable or fruit combinations.
Preparation time: a few minutes · No cooking · Makes ½ teacup.

4 tablespoons salad oil
2 tablespoons white vinegar
2 tablespoons pineapple syrup *or* orange squash
½ teaspoon salt
a little pepper powder

Mix all the ingredients in a bottle and shake vigorously.

FACING PAGE
1 ORANGE CASTLES
2 STRAWBERRY GLAZE CREAM PIE
3 THOUSAND ISLAND DRESSING
4 WINTER SOUP WITH RICE AND CHEESE BALLS
5 STUFFED POTATOES WITH CORN

LEMON JELLY ASPIC SALAD PICTURE ON FACING PAGE

Impressive and elegant.
Preparation time: 10 minutes · Setting time: 30 minutes · Serves 10.

1 small can (450 grams)
   pineapple slices
2 teacups mixed boiled
   vegetables (french beans,
   carrots, green peas)
2 chopped cucumbers
1 capsicum cut into small pieces
sugar and salt to taste
lettuce leaves for decoration

For the jelly
1 packet (100 grams) lemon jelly
2 teaspoons lemon juice
3 teaspoons sugar
1 teaspoon salt

For the cream
200 grams (7 oz.) fresh cream
3 teaspoons powdered sugar
1 teaspoon mustard powder
1 teaspoon salt

1. Drain the pineapple slices and chop finely.
2. Dissolve the jelly in 3 teacups of boiling water. Cool a little and add the lemon juice, sugar and salt. Pour a little jelly into a wet mould and put to set in the refrigerator.
3. Beat the cream until thick. Add the sugar, mustard powder and salt and mix well.
4. Mix the remaining jelly with the cream, vegetables, cucumbers, capsicum and pineapple. Add sugar and salt and pour over the set jelly. Put to set in the refrigerator.
5. Just before serving, dip the mould in hot water for a few seconds, loosen the sides and unmould on a plate.

★ Serve cold surrounded by lettuce leaves.

Note: If you like, you can also serve with green goddess dressing.

FRESH CURD SALAD CREAM

Serve with combinations of fruits and boiled vegetables.
Preparation time: a few minutes · No cooking · Makes 1 teacup.

200 grams (7 oz.) fresh cream
3 tablespoons thick curds
2 teaspoons powdered sugar
1 teaspoon mustard powder
1 teaspoon salt

1. Beat the cream until thick.
2. Add the remaining ingredients and mix well.

FACING PAGE
1 CHOCOLATE AND VANILLA GATEAU
2 LEMON JELLY ASPIC SALAD
3 STACKED PANCAKES
4 ONION AND PEA SOUP

FRESH CURD THOUSAND ISLAND DRESSING

Too good is the only word for this delicious dressing without oil.
Serve with jelly salads and fresh fruits or as a dip.
Preparation time: a few minutes · No cooking · Makes 1¼ teacups.

200 grams (7 oz.) fresh cream
3 tablespoons thick curds
3 tablespoons tomato ketchup
½ teaspoon chilli sauce
2 teaspoons chopped onion
2 teaspoons chopped capsicum
¼ teaspoon chopped green
   chillies
1 level teaspoon mustard
   powder
1 tablespoon powdered sugar
salt to taste

1. Beat the cream until thick.
2. Add the remaining ingredients and mix well.
3. Chill and store in the refrigerator.

YOGHURT DRESSING

An interesting alternative to mayonnaise. Goes very well with macaroni and cucumber.
Preparation time: a few minutes · No cooking · Makes 2 teacups.

3 teacups fresh curds
2 teaspoons chopped capsicum
2 teaspoons chopped onions
1 chopped green chilli
2 tablespoons fresh cream
salt to taste

1. Tie the curds in a thin cloth and hang for 2 hours to allow the water to drain out.
2. To the thickened curds, add the capsicum, onions, chilli, cream and salt.

★ Serve cold.

ORANGE CREAM DRESSING

Delicately flavoured with orange, good with fruit combination.
Preparation time: a few minutes · No cooking · Makes 1 teacup.

200 grams (7 oz.) fresh cream
3 tablespoons orange squash
½ teaspoon lemon juice
1 level teaspoon mustard
   powder
½ teaspoon salt
½ teaspoon sugar

1. Beat the cream.
2. Add the remaining ingredients and mix well.

GREEN GODDESS DRESSING

Cool and pleasing, beautifully green.
Preparation time: a few minutes · No cooking · Makes 1 teacup.

2 teacups fresh curds
2 to 3 tablespoons fresh cream
1 tablespoon chopped parsley
1 chopped spring onion
1 chopped green chilli
1 teaspoon chopped capsicum
2 teaspoons sugar
a few drops green colouring

1. Tie the curds in a piece of thin cloth and hang for 1 hour to allow the water to drain out.
2. Mix with all the other ingredients.

Note: When making this dressing for dieting salads, use thicker curds made from skimmed milk and instead of fresh cream, use 2 tablespoons of skimmed milk.

FRUIT AND JELLY SALAD

A colourful touch to the party. A trio of fruits and flavours.
Preparation time: 15 minutes · Setting time: 40 minutes · Serves 10.

1 packet (100 grams) lemon or
  orange jelly
¾ teacup sliced grapes
1 tablespoon chopped
  capsicum
1 tablespoon chopped celery
2 sliced bananas
juice of 1 lemon
3 teaspoons powdered sugar
1 teaspoon salt
1 teacup sliced strawberries or
  other fruit
red and green colouring
lettuce leaves, shredded
  cabbage and grated carrots
  for decoration
yoghurt dressing, page 38,
  to serve

1. Dissolve the jelly in 3 teacups of boiling water. Cool a little and add the lemon juice, sugar and salt.
2. Divide the jelly into 3 equal parts. Keep one part as it is. To the other parts, add red and green colouring respectively.
3. Put the green coloured jelly to set in the refrigerator.
4. When it sets partially, add the grapes, capsicum and celery. Mix well and pour into any fancy jelly mould or ring mould. Put to set in the refrigerator.
5. Put the red coloured jelly to set in the refrigerator.
6. When it sets partially, add the strawberries. Mix well and pour over the set green jelly. Put to set in the refrigerator.
7. Put the uncoloured jelly to set in the refrigerator.
8. When it sets partially, add the bananas. Mix well and pour over the set jelly portions. Put to set in the refrigerator.
9. To serve, dip the mould in hot water for a few seconds, loosen the sides and unmould on a plate.
10. Fill the centre with yoghurt dressing.

★ Decorate with lettuce leaves, shredded cabbage and grated carrots and serve cold.

BREAD AND BEAN SALAD PICTURE ON PAGE 81

Your guests will love this unusual combination of Eastern chutney and Western dressing.
Preparation time: 15 minutes · No cooking · Serves 10.

1 bread loaf
1 large can (450 grams) baked beans
4 to 5 tablespoons green chutney
2 teacups grated carrots and cabbage, 1 sliced apple and a few walnuts for decoration

To be mixed into a dressing
¼ can (of a 400 grams full can) condensed milk
½ tablespoon salad oil
2 tablespoons white vinegar
¼ teaspoon salt
1 tablespoon milk
1 teaspoon lemon juice
½ teaspoon mustard powder

1. Remove the crust from the bread slices.
2. Divide each slice into two and apply chutney on one side.
3. Fill a serving plate with bread slices, placing the chutney side on the bottom.
4. Spread the baked beans on the bread pieces.
5. Spread the dressing over the beans.
6. Decorate with grated carrots and cabbage on the sides. Put apple slices in the centre and sprinkle walnuts on top.

★ Serve cold.

Note: If you are in a hurry, you can use mayonnaise as a dressing in place of the above.

MACARONI CUCUMBER SALAD

Yoghurt enlivens this simple salad.
Preparation time: 15 minutes · No cooking · Serves 10.

2 teacups boiled ring macaroni
3 large cucumbers, finely chopped
1 teacup fresh cream
1½ teacups thick curds
1 teaspoon mustard powder
2 chopped green chillies
3 to 4 teaspoons powdered sugar
salt to taste
capsicum slices, cucumber slices and salad leaves for decoration

1. Beat the cream until thick.
2. Add the curds, mustard powder, green chillies, sugar and salt and mix well.
3. Add the macaroni and cucumbers and mix well.
4. Fill the salad in a jelly mould or a bowl and chill for 2 hours.
5. To serve, unmould on a serving plate.

★ Decorate with capsicum slices, cucumber slices and salad leaves and serve cold.

PEACH AND MELON SALAD

This sparkling yellow and red salad will dazzle your guests.
Preparation time: 10 minutes · Setting time: 30 minutes · Serves 10.

1 packet (100 grams) pineapple *or* orange jelly
1 small can (450 grams) peaches
2 to 3 teacups water-melon pieces
1 teaspoon lemon juice
1 teaspoon sugar
½ teaspoon salt
½ teacup shredded cabbage
½ teacup grated carrots
sugar, salt and pepper to taste
chopped lettuce, grated carrots and shredded cabbage for decoration
fresh curd Thousand Island dressing, *page 38, or* green goddess dressing, *page 39,* to serve

1. Dissolve the jelly in 3 teacups of boiling water. Cool a little and add the lemon juice, sugar and salt.
2. Pour a little jelly into a wet ring mould.
3. Arrange a few peach and melon pieces decoratively in the jelly and put to set in the refrigerator.
4. Pour the remaining jelly into a broad vessel and put to set in the refrigerator.
5. When it sets partially, add the cabbage, carrots, 1 teacup of melon pieces, the rest of the peaches (chopped), sugar, salt and pepper.
6. Mix well and pour over the set jelly. Put to set in the refrigerator.
7. Just before serving, dip the mould in hot water for a few seconds, loosen the sides and unmould on a plate.
8. Surround with crisp cabbage, lettuce and carrots.

★ Fill the centre with fresh curds Thousand Island dressing and serve cold.

BANANA PANEER SALAD

Nutritious and delicious.
Preparation time: 10 minutes · No cooking · Serves 8.

6 bananas
5 tablespoons fresh curd salad cream, *page 37*
4 tablespoons crumbled paneer *or* cottage cheese
1 tablespoon chopped walnuts *or* chopped roasted peanuts
lettuce leaves and grated carrots for decoration

1. Slit the bananas.
2. Mix the cream with the paneer and nuts.
3. Pile this mixture over the bananas.
4. Chill for 10 minutes.
5. Put on lettuce leaves, sprinkle grated carrots on top.

★ Serve chilled.

Note: If fresh curds are not available, you can use ordinary salad cream.

CABBAGE AND JELLY SALAD

Light and refreshing.
Preparation time: 10 minutes · Setting time: 30 minutes · Serves 8 to 10.

1 packet (100 grams) lemon jelly
1½ teacups grated cabbage
½ teacup chopped celery
4 tablespoons sliced capsicum
3 tablespoons grated onions
½ teacup mayonnaise
3 to 4 tablespoons white
    vinegar
salt and pepper to taste
lettuce leaves for decoration
green goddess dressing,
    page 39, to serve.

1. Dissolve the jelly in 3 teacups of boiling water.
2. Cool a little and add the vinegar, salt and pepper.
3. Mix the vegetables and mayonnaise and add to the jelly.
4. Pour into a wet mould and put to set in the refrigerator.
5. Just before serving, dip the mould in hot water for a few seconds, loosen the sides and unmould on a plate.

★ Surround with lettuce leaves and serve cold with green goddess dressing.

JIFFY FRUIT AND VEGETABLE SALAD

PICTURE ON PAGE 65

A quick salad for the health-conscious.
Preparation time: 10 minutes · No cooking · Serves 10.

2 to 3 teacups water-melon
    pieces
1 small can (450 grams)
    pineapple titbits
1 teacup grapes
1 head celery
2 cucumbers
2 capsicums
sugar, salt and pepper to taste
fruity french dressing, *page 34,*
    or Thousand Island dressing,
    page 165, to serve.

1. Cut the vegetables into big pieces.
2. Mix the fruit and vegetable pieces. Add sugar, salt and pepper and mix well.
3. Chill for 2 hours.

★ Serve with fruity french dressing.

PINEAPPLE OUTRIGGER PICTURE ON FACING PAGE

An extra-special hearty fruit salad served with a delicate orange flavoured dressing.
Preparation time: 20 minutes · No cooking · Serves 10.

1 large ripe pineapple
3 teacups mixed chopped fruits
   (grapes, bananas, oranges,
   apples)
1 tablespoon chopped celery
1½ teacups orange cream
   dressing, *page 39*
grated carrots, grapes and
   strawberries for decoration

1. Divide the pineapple into 2 parts and scoop out
   the centre. Chop the scooped portion of the
   pineapple.
2. Mix with the other fruits.
3. Add the celery and chill.

How to serve
   Fill the pineapple halves with alternate layers
   of the fruit mixture and orange cream.

   ★ Decorate with grated carrots, grapes and
   strawberries and serve cold.

TOSSED SALAD

An economical and tasty everyday salad.
Preparation time: 20 minutes · Cooking time: 10 minutes · Serves 8.

500 grams (1⅛ lb.) white
   pumpkin
2 sliced onions
2 sliced capsicums
3 carrots
3 tomatoes
salt and pepper to taste
french dressing to serve

1. Cut the pumpkin and carrots like matchsticks.
2. Put in boiling water and cook for 2 to 3
   minutes. Drain.
3. Slice the tomatoes and remove the pulp.
4. Mix all the ingredients and chill for 2 hours.
5. Just before serving, add salt and pepper and
   mix well.

   ★ Pour french dressing on top and serve.

   Note: If you like, also add bean sprouts.

FACING PAGE
1 PINEAPPLE OUTRIGGER
2 STRAWBERRY CARNIVAL PUDDING
3 ORANGE AND LEMON DRINK
4 STRAWBERRY AND PINEAPPLE SLICE

V. Indian Dishes

STUFFED TOMATOES WITH PANEER AND VEGETABLES PICTURE ON FACING PAGE

Colourful, tempting and tasty.
Preparation time: 15 minutes · Cooking time: 25 minutes · Serves 5.

10 small tomatoes
150 grams (6 oz.) crumbled
   paneer or khoya
2 teacups mixed boiled
   vegetables (french beans,
   carrots, green peas)
1 chopped onion
2 chopped green chillies
2 tablespoons chopped
   cashewnuts
2 tablespoons ghee
salt to taste

For the gravy
2 grated onions
3 tablespoons tomato ketchup
½ teaspoon chilli powder
2 tablespoons ghee
salt to taste

For the tomatoes
1. Scoop the tomatoes. Keep aside the pulp for the gravy.
2. Add the ghee and fry the onion for 1 minute.
3. Add the green chillies and fry again for ½ minute.
4. Add the cashewnuts and fry again for ½ minute.
5. Add the vegetables, paneer and salt and cook for a few minutes.
6. Fill the tomatoes with the mixture.

For the gravy
1. Heat the ghee and fry the onion till golden in colour.
2. Add the tomato pulp, tomato ketchup, chilli powder and salt and boil for 1 minute.

How to proceed
1. Grease a flat baking tray and arrange the tomatoes over it.
2. Pour the gravy all over and bake in a hot oven at 400°F for 15 to 20 minutes.

★ Serve hot. If you like, decorate with potato wafers.

Note: You can substitute the mixed boiled vegetables by boiled green peas.

FACING PAGE
1 BAKED KHICHADI
2 STUFFED TOMATOES WITH PANEER AND VEGETABLES
3 MASOOR DAL WITH SPINACH
4 TOMATO RASAM
5 METHI PALAK AUR MAKKI KI ROTI

TOMATO RASAM PICTURE ON PAGE 46

A quick and appetising South Indian rasam without dal.
Preparation time: 5 minutes · Cooking time: 25 minutes · Serves 8.

3 large tomatoes
3 tablespoons tamarind water
1 teaspoon lemon juice
¼ teaspoon turmeric powder
1 teaspoon dhana-jira powder
½ teaspoon chilli powder
¼ teaspoon asafoetida
1 tablespoon ghee

To be ground dry into a masala powder
1 teaspoon cumin seeds
1½ teaspoons coriander seeds
8 peppercorns

1. Boil 8 glasses of water.
2. Add the whole tomatoes, tamarind water, lemon juice, turmeric powder, dhana-jira powder, chilli powder, asafoetida and masala powder and boil for a further 10 minutes.
3. Break the tomatoes with a spoon.
4. Boil again for 10 minutes.
5. Add the ghee.

★ Serve the liquid hot, taking care not to serve the tomatoes.

MASOOR DAL WITH SPINACH PICTURE ON PAGE 46

You will like this combination of spinach and lentils.
Preparation time: 10 minutes · Cooking time: 20 minutes · Serves 6 to 8.

1½ teacups uncooked masoor dal
1½ teacups chopped spinach
1 chopped onion
1 teaspoon cumin seeds
2 teaspoons amchur powder
1 chopped tomato
½ teaspoon turmeric powder
¾ teaspoon chilli powder
3 tablespoons ghee
salt to taste

To be ground into a paste
6 cloves garlic
6 green chillies
25 mm. (1") piece ginger

1. Cook the dal separately with 2 teacups of water.
2. Heat 1½ tablespoons of ghee, add the onion and cumin seeds and fry for at least 2 minutes.
3. Add the cooked dal, the spinach, amchur powder, tomato, turmeric powder, paste and salt and boil for a few minutes.
4. Just before serving, heat the remaining ghee and the chilli powder and pour immediately over the mixture.

★ Serve hot.

BAKED PANEER WITH SPINACH IN TOMATO GRAVY

An Indian dish cooked with a Western touch.
Preparation time: 20 minutes · Cooking time: 20 minutes · Serves 6 to 8.

500 grams (1⅛ lb.) paneer
3 tablespoons grated cheese
ghee for deep frying

1. Cut the paneer into long thin pieces.
2. Deep fry lightly in ghee.

For the spinach

6 teacups chopped spinach
1 chopped onion
2 teaspoons plain flour
3 chopped green chillies
2 tablespoons fresh cream
¼ teaspoon nutmeg
1 tablespoon ghee
salt to taste

For the spinach

1. Cook the spinach without adding any water. If you like, add a pinch of soda bi-carb while cooking.
2. When cooked, blend in a liquidiser.
3. Heat the ghee and fry the onion for ½ minute.
4. Add the flour and fry again for ½ minute.
5. Add the green chillies, spinach and salt and cook for 1 minute.
6. Add the nutmeg.
7. Switch off the gas. Add the cream.

For the tomato gravy

4 tomatoes
1 chopped onion
2 cloves crushed garlic (optional)
½ teaspoon chilli powder
1 teaspoon sugar (approx.)
1 tablespoon ghee or oil
salt to taste

For the tomato gravy

1. Cut the tomatoes into big pieces.
2. Heat the ghee and fry the onion and garlic for 1 minute.
3. Add the tomatoes and cook until they are soft.
4. Blend in a liquidiser.
5. Add the chilli powder, sugar and salt and boil for 2 to 3 minutes.

How to serve

1. Spread a few paneer pieces on a greased baking dish. Spread half the spinach mixture on the paneer. Make similar layers with some more paneer pieces and the balance spinach mixture.
2. Cover with the remaining paneer slices and spread the tomato gravy on top. Cover with grated cheese.
3. Bake in a hot oven at 400°F for 15 to 20 minutes.

   ★ Serve hot.

PUNJABI MALAI PALAK

Nourishing and tasty, quick to prepare.
Preparation time: 10 minutes · Cooking time: 20 minutes · Serves 6 to 8.

100 grams (4 oz.) moong dal
  (with skin)
3 teacups chopped spinach
25 mm. (1") piece finely
  chopped ginger
2 finely chopped green chillies
½ teaspoon turmeric powder
1 finely chopped onion
½ teaspoon chilli powder
3 to 4 tablespoons fresh curds
2 tablespoons ghee
salt to taste

1. Wash the moong dal thoroughly.
2. Mix the moong dal, spinach, ginger, green chillies and turmeric powder. Add 2 teacups of water and cook.
3. When cooked, the dal should be thick and soft. Mash well.
4. Heat the ghee and fry the onion for 1 minute. Add the chilli powder and fry for ½ minute.
5. Add the dal and salt. Cook for 3 to 4 minutes.
6. Beat the curds and add to the mixture. Add a little water so that the mixture looks like a thick cream.

★ Serve hot with parathas.

SHAHI CAULIFLOWER

Rich and tasty.
Preparation time: 20 minutes · Cooking time: 10 minutes · Serves 6 to 8.

500 grams (1⅛ lb.) cauliflower
8 to 10 small potatoes
6 to 7 small tomatoes
1 teacup boiled green peas
1 teacup fresh curds
2 tablespoons fresh cream
½ teaspoon sugar
2 tablespoons ghee
salt to taste
ghee for deep frying

To be ground into a paste
8 Kashmiri chillies
8 cloves garlic
25 mm. (1") piece ginger
½ teaspoon turmeric powder
2 large onions
4 teaspoons khus-khus

1. Cut the cauliflower into big pieces and deep fry in ghee.
2. Similarly, deep fry the potatoes in ghee.
3. Beat the curds.
4. Heat the ghee and fry the paste. Add the beaten curds and 1 teacup of water. Add the fried cauliflower and potatoes, tomatoes, green peas and salt.
5. Cover and cook for a few minutes.
6. Add the cream and sugar and mix well.

★ Sprinkle a little garam masala on top and serve hot.

MASALA VEGETABLES WITH COCONUT SAUCE

Vegetables presented in a different and unusual way.
Preparation time: 15 minutes · Cooking time: 25 minutes · Serves 6 to 8.

4 teacups mixed chopped vegetables (cabbage, carrots, potatoes, french beans)
1 teacup cooked corn
1 chopped onion
2 pinches soda bi-carb
2 tablespoons ghee
3 tablespoons plain flour
½ teaspoon turmeric powder
1 tablespoon chopped coriander
4 to 5 finely chopped green chillies
2 sliced tomatoes
1 sliced capsicum
1 tablespoon oil
salt to taste

1. Heat the ghee and fry the onion for 1 minute.
2. Add the vegetables, turmeric powder, soda bi-carb and salt.
3. Cover and cook gently until soft.
4. Sprinkle the flour all over the vegetables.
5. Mix well and cook again for 2 minutes.
6. Add the corn, coriander, green chillies and salt.
7. Grease a ring mould tin about 175 mm. (7") in diameter. Heat the oil, pour into the tin and spread the tomato and capsicum slices on the bottom.
8. Fill the tin with the mixture.
9. Bake in a hot oven at 400°F for 10 minutes.
10. Turn upside down on a serving plate.

★ Serve hot with or without coconut sauce.

COCONUT SAUCE

An attractive and tasty accompaniment to pullavs.
Preparation time: a few minutes · Cooking time: a few minutes · Makes 4 teacups.

1 large coconut
1 slit green chilli
2 curry leaves
2 tablespoons chopped coriander
1 teaspoon cumin seeds
a pinch sugar (optional)
1 tablespoon ghee or oil
salt to taste

1. Grate the coconut, add 3 teacups of hot water and allow to stand for a little while. Blend in a liquidiser and strain.
2. Heat the ghee and fry the cumin seeds for ½ minute.
3. Add the chilli and curry leaves and fry again for a little while.
4. Add the coconut, sugar and salt.

★ Serve warm taking care not to boil.

STUFFED CAULIFLOWER PURIS

Coconut and groundnut make these puris unusual and special.
Preparation time: 20 minutes · Cooking time: 30 minutes · Makes about 15 puris.

For the dough
3 teacups whole meal flour
½ teaspoon salt
½ teaspoon turmeric powder
(optional)
1 tablespoon ghee

To be mixed into a stuffing mixture
2 teacups finely grated
cauliflower
¾ teacup grated fresh coconut
½ teacup coarsely pounded
roasted groundnuts
6 chopped green chillies
2 tablespoons chopped
coriander
salt to taste

For deep frying
ghee *or* oil

For serving
sweet and sour sauce

For the sweet and sour sauce
10 to 12 slit green chillies
½ teacup jaggery (gur)
3 tablespoons tamarind
½ teaspoon mustard seeds
1 teaspoon fenugreek seeds
1 tablespoon oil
salt to taste

For the dough
1. Mix all the ingredients and add enough water
   to make a soft dough.
2. Knead for 5 minutes.
3. Roll out small puris.

How to proceed
1. Spread a little stuffing mixture on one puri and
   put another on top.
2. Stick the edges, applying a little water if
   necessary. Repeat with the remaining puris.
3. Deep fry in ghee.

★ Serve hot with the sweet and sour sauce.

For the sweet and sour sauce
1. Soak the tamarind in ¾ teacup of water.
   Strain and take out tamarind water.
2. Mix the tamarind water, jaggery and green
   chillies. Boil on a low flame for a few minutes.
3. Heat the oil and add the mustard seeds and
   fenugreek seeds. Cook until the fenugreek
   seeds become red. Pour over the sauce.
4. Boil again for 2 minutes.
5. Cool.

★ Serve with stuffed cauliflower puris.

METHI PALAK AUR MAKKI KI ROTI PICTURE ON PAGE 46

Methi and palak add taste to the traditional makki roti.
Preparation time: 10 minutes · Cooking time: 20 minutes · Makes about 8 to 10 rotis.

250 grams (9 oz.) maize flour
1 teacup chopped spinach
½ teacup chopped fenugreek
   leaves (methi bhaji)
½ teaspoon chilli powder
2 finely chopped green chillies
½ teaspoon salt
ghee for serving

1. Mix the maize flour, spinach, fenugreek leaves, chilli powder, green chillies and salt. Add hot water and make a soft dough.
2. Divide the dough into 6 or 7 parts.
3. Spread a damp cloth on a wooden board and flatten one part until it is 150 to 175 mm. (6" to 7") in diameter.
4. Lift with the cloth and put it upside down on a tava. Remove the cloth.
5. Cook on both sides, using a little ghee if desired. Repeat for the remaining dough.

★ Serve hot with ghee.

MASALA PANEER MUTTER

An enjoyable version of the traditional Punjabi dish.
Preparation time: 20 minutes · Cooking time: 10 minutes · Serves 6 to 8.

For the paste
2 sliced onions
2 teaspoons coriander seeds
1 teaspoon cumin seeds
1½ teaspoons chilli powder
¼ teaspoon turmeric powder
1 tablespoon khus-khus
3 cloves
3 peppercorns
3 sticks cinnamon
3 tablespoons oil

Other ingredients
2 teacups boiled green peas
1 teacup fried paneer cubes
3 tablespoons tomato ketchup
3 tablespoons ghee
salt to taste
garam masala and chopped
   coriander for decoration

For the paste
1. Heat the oil and fry the onions and the spices for 1 minute.
2. Grind into a paste with the help of water.

How to proceed
1. Heat the ghee and fry the paste for 1 minute.
2. Add the tomato ketchup and fry for a little while.
3. Add the green peas, paneer, salt and ½ teacup of water and boil for a few minutes.

★ Sprinkle garam masala and coriander on top and serve hot.

53

MASALA BAKED CORN

Corn spiced with coriander, green chillies and tomato sauce.
Preparation time: 10 minutes · Cooking time: 25 minutes · Serves 6 to 8.

2½ teacups cooked tender corn
1 chopped onion
4 chopped green chillies
1 tablespoon butter
1 teacup milk
½ teacup fresh cream
½ teacup fresh curds
1 tablespoon plain flour
3 tablespoons chopped
   coriander
salt to taste
buttered toast pieces for
   decoration

For the sauce
4 tablespoons tomato ketchup
1 teaspoon plain flour
1 teaspoon butter

For the topping
4 tablespoons grated cooking
   cheese

1. Heat the butter and fry the onion for 1 minute. Add the green chillies and fry for a few seconds.
2. Add the corn and salt.
3. Mix the milk, cream, curds and flour very well and add to the corn mixture.
4. Cook for a few minutes.
5. Add the coriander.
6. Prepare the sauce by heating the butter, frying the flour and adding the tomato ketchup and 2 tablespoons of water. Cook for 1 minute.
7. Spread the corn mixture in a greased baking dish. Cover with the sauce and sprinkle the cheese on top.
8. Bake in a hot oven at 450°F for 20 minutes.

★ Decorate with pieces of buttered toast and serve.

Note: You can also directly spread the corn mixture on buttered toast pieces, cover with the sauce, sprinkle cheese and either bake as above or grill.

VEGETABLE DO PYAZ

A popular and tasty vegetable.
Preparation time: 20 minutes · Cooking time: 20 minutes · Serves 6 to 8.

250 grams (9 oz.) cauliflower
250 grams (9 oz.) french beans
250 grams (9 oz.) tomatoes
250 grams (9 oz.) carrots
1 teacup green peas
2 sliced onions
2 tablespoons fresh cream
½ teaspoon sugar
3 tablespoons ghee
salt to taste

1. Cut the vegetables into square pieces.
2. Heat the ghee and fry the sliced onions until golden brown in colour.
3. Remove the onions.
4. Using the same ghee, fry the paste for 2 to 3 minutes.
5. Add the vegetables and fry again for 1 minute.
6. Add the browned onions and 1 teacup of water.

To be ground into a paste

10 Kashmiri chillies (without
    seeds)
2 teaspoons coriander seeds
¼ teaspoon turmeric powder
1 teaspoon cumin seeds
25 mm. (1″) piece ginger
4 cloves garlic
½ teaspoon mustard seeds
1 onion

7. Cook until the vegetables are tender and the
   gravy is thick. Add the cream, sugar and salt
   and mix well.

★ Serve hot.

PANEER MAKHANA KORMA

Make this dish when you are short of vegetables.
Preparation time: 10 minutes · Cooking time: 15 minutes · Serves 6 to 8.

200 grams (7 oz.) paneer,
    cut into cubes
200 grams (7 oz.) makhana
100 grams (4 oz.) khoya
2 tablespoons fresh curds
½ teaspoon chilli powder
3 tablespoons tomato ketchup
1 tablespoon cashewnuts
1 tablespoon melted butter
salt to taste
oil for frying
chopped coriander for
    garnishing

To be ground into a paste
3 teaspoons khus-khus
2 tablespoons cashewnuts

1. Fry the paneer lightly in oil.
2. Similarly, fry the makhanas lightly in oil.
3. Mix the khoya, curds and paste.
4. Heat the butter, add the khoya mixture and
   sprinkle a little water to make it a smooth
   paste. Fry for 2 to 3 minutes.
5. Add the fried makhanas, chilli powder, tomato
   ketchup and salt and cook for a few minutes.
6. Add a little water. Add the cashewnuts.

★ Sprinkle chopped coriander on top and
serve hot.

GREEN PEA DHOKLAS

Something different. Quick and easy to prepare.
Preparation time: 10 minutes · Cooking time: 15 minutes · Serves 3 to 4.

For the batter
¾ teacup green peas
3 green chillies
1½ teacups gram flour
a pinch asafoetida
½ teaspoon sugar
1 teaspoon salt
a few drops green colouring

For fermenting
½ teaspoon sugar
¼ teaspoon soda bi-carb
½ teaspoon citric acid
¾ teaspoon fruit salt

For tempering (baghaar)
(only half quantity required)
¾ teaspoon mustard seeds
2 pinches asafoetida
3 to 4 slit green chillies (washed twice)
½ teacup water
½ teaspoon lemon juice
½ teaspoon sugar
½ teaspoon salt
1½ tablespoons oil

For decoration
chopped coriander and grated coconut

For serving
green chutney

For the batter
1. Blend the green peas and green chillies with 3 tablespoons of water in a liquidiser.
2. Mix the remaining ingredients for the batter with the green peas mixture. Add a little water to make it look like a thick sauce. Beat for ½ minute.
3. Heat a thali (flat metal plate with low rim) on which a little oil has been applied.
4. Put the ingredients for fermenting in a vessel and sprinkle 1 tablespoon of water on top.
5. Mix the batter very well and pour on the hot thali.
6. Steam for 5 to 7 minutes. Cool.

For tempering (baghaar)
1. Heat the oil and fry the mustard seeds for a few seconds.
2. Switch off the fire.
3. After a little while, add the asafoetida and green chillies.
4. After a little while, add the water, lemon juice, sugar and salt and mix well.

How to serve
When you want to serve, spread half the tempering mixture over the dhoklas and steam again for a few minutes. Cut into diamond pieces, sprinkle coriander and grated coconut on top and serve with green chutney.

BAKED GREEN RICE WITH SPINACH PAKODAS

A meal by itself.
Preparation time: 20 minutes · Cooking time: 30 minutes · Serves 6.

For the rice
1½ teacups uncooked rice
1 teacup boiled green peas
2 sticks cinnamon
2 cloves
2 cardamoms
3 tablespoons ghee
salt to taste

**To be ground into a paste
    (for the rice)**
1 onion
8 cloves garlic
7 green chillies
25 mm. (1") piece ginger
1 tablespoon khus-khus
2 teacups chopped coriander
juice of ½ lemon

For the spinach pakodas
4 teacups chopped spinach
3 chopped green chillies
3 tablespoons gram flour
2 pinches soda bi-carb
salt to taste
oil for deep frying

For the curry
1 coconut
1 teaspoon plain flour
2 teaspoons chutney
1 teaspoon cumin seeds
2 pinches sugar
1 tablespoon ghee
salt to taste

For the rice
1. Boil the rice. Each grain of the cooked rice should be separate. Drain and cool.
2. Heat the ghee and fry the paste, cinnamon, cloves and cardamoms for at least 3 to 4 minutes.
3. Add the rice, green peas and salt and cook for 1 minute.

For the spinach pakodas
1. Boil the spinach. When cooked, drain thoroughly and grind or chop very finely.
2. Add the green chillies, gram flour, soda bi-carb and salt. Mix well and make small balls of the mixture.
3. Deep fry in oil.

For the curry
1. Grate the coconut, add 2 teacups of water and allow to stand for a little while. Blend in a liquidiser and pass through a sieve to get thick coconut milk.
2. Heat the ghee and fry the cumin seeds for ½ minute.
3. Add the plain flour and chutney and fry again for ½ minute.
4. Add the coconut milk, sugar and salt and boil for 2 minutes.

How to proceed
Spread half the rice on a large piece of aluminium foil. Pour curry on the rice and put half the pakodas on top. Make a second such layer with the remaining rice, curry and pakodas. Cover with another aluminium foil and bake in a hot oven at 450°F for 25 minutes.

★ Serve hot.

BAKED KHICHADI PICTURE ON PAGE 46

A balanced meal by itself.
Preparation time: 20 minutes · Cooking time: 1 hour · Serves 8.

For the khichadi
2 teacups uncooked rice
¾ teacup toovar dal
¼ teaspoon turmeric powder
2 cloves
2 sticks cinnamon
2 cardamoms
2 bay leaves
2 tablespoons ghee
salt to taste

For the curry
3 tomatoes
2 grated onions
2 teaspoons dhana-jira powder
2 teaspoons chilli powder
¼ teaspoon turmeric powder
3 teacups mixed boiled
    vegetables (french beans,
    carrots, potatoes, green peas)
2 tablespoons fresh cream
2 cardamoms
3 tablespoons ghee
salt to taste

**To be ground into a paste
    (for the curry)**
4 cloves garlic
25 mm. (1″) piece ginger

For baking
2 tablespoons ghee

For decoration
papad and sago vadis (optional)

For the khichadi
1. Heat the ghee and fry the cloves, cinnamon, cardamoms and bay leaves for a few seconds.
2. Add the rice and dal and cook for 2 to 3 minutes.
3. Add 5 teacups of water, the turmeric powder and salt.
4. Cover and cook until soft.

For the curry
1. Put the tomatoes in hot water. After 10 minutes, take off the skin and chop.
2. Heat the ghee and fry the grated onions until light pink in colour.
3. Add the paste and cardamoms and fry again for 1 minute.
4. Add the dhana-jira, chilli and turmeric powders and fry again for ½ minute.
5. Add tomatoes and fry for 2 to 3 minutes.
6. Add the vegetables and salt and cook for 3 to 4 minutes.
7. Add the cream and mix well.

How to proceed
1. Spread the ghee at the bottom of a well-greased bowl.
2. Make layers of khichadi and vegetables and press well.
3. Cover with a tight lid and bake in a hot oven at 450°F for 25 to 30 minutes.
4. To serve, turn upside down.

★ Decorate with papad or sago vadis and serve hot with kadhi or buttermilk.

58

RICE AND CURRY IN BANANA LEAF

Banana leaf gives a special delicate flavour to this rice.
Preparation time: 20 minutes · Cooking time: 40 minutes · Makes 10 to 12 packets.

For the rice
2 teacups uncooked rice
½ teaspoon shah-jira
1 tablespoon ghee
salt to taste

For the curry
2 tablespoons tomato pureé
1 tablespoon fresh cream
2 tablespoons ghee
salt to taste

**To be ground into a paste
(for the curry)**
1 onion
2 tablespoons grated coconut
5 red chillies
2 teaspoons coriander seeds
1 teaspoon cumin seeds
2 cardamoms
12 mm. (½") piece ginger
3 cloves garlic

For the rice
1. Boil the rice. Each grain of the cooked rice should be separate. Drain and cool.
2. Heat the ghee and fry the shah-jira. Add the rice and salt.

For the curry
1. Heat the ghee and fry the paste for 3 to 4 minutes.
2. Add the tomato pureé, cream and salt and cook for 1 minute.

How to proceed
1. Cut banana leaves into medium-sized squares. In each square, spread one portion of rice and then spread a little curry. Fold the individual leaves and fasten with toothpicks.
2. Steam the packets for at least 15 minutes.

★ Serve hot.

Note: You can pack the rice and curry in aluminium foil if banana leaves are not available.

PANEER SPROUTED MATH BIRYANI

A lentil rice cooked in spicy coconut milk.
Preparation time: 15 minutes · Cooking time: 30 minutes · Serves 6 to 8.

1 teacup uncooked rice
2 teacups sprouted math
1 potato cut into small pieces
1 carrot cut into small pieces
1 tomato cut into small pieces
200 grams (7 oz.) paneer
1 tablespoon raisins
1 tablespoon cashewnuts
4 tablespoons ghee
1 teacup fresh curds
salt to taste

For the coconut milk
½ coconut
1 teaspoon cumin seeds
½ teaspoon turmeric powder
1 onion
6 red chillies

1. Mix all the ingredients for the coconut milk, add 2 teacups of water and blend in a liquidiser. Strain.
2. Heat 2 tablespoons of ghee and fry the raisins and cashewnuts until light brown. Keep aside the fried raisins and nuts.
3. To the same ghee, add the math, potato, carrot and salt. Cover and cook until it is three-quarter cooked.
4. Heat the remaining ghee. Add the rice and fry for a few minutes.
5. Add the coconut milk, tomato and salt. Cover and cook.
6. When the rice is three-quarter done, add the cooked vegetables, paneer and curds. Cover and cook again for a few minutes.
7. When done, mix well.

   ★ Serve hot garnished with the fried raisins and nuts.

MASALA BHAAT

A delicious combination of rice and Gujarati style sabji.
Preparation time: 20 minutes · Cooking time: 40 minutes · Serves 6 to 8.

1½ teacups uncooked rice
5 brinjals
5 onions
5 small potatoes
5 to 6 small tondlies (optional)
1 teacup boiled green peas
5 tablespoons oil
salt to taste

1. Boil the rice. Each grain of the cooked rice should be separate. Drain and cool.
2. Make 4 vertical slits in the brinjals, onions, potatoes and tondlies and stuff with the masala mixture. A little mixture will be left over.
3. Heat the oil, add the stuffed vegetables and salt and very little water. Pressure cook or cover and cook until soft.

To be mixed together into a masala mixture

½ grated coconut
4 teaspoons dhana-jira powder
1 teaspoon sugar
2 teaspoons chilli powder
1 teaspoon garam masala
1½ teacups chopped coriander
a pinch asafoetida
salt to taste

4. Mix the cooked rice, remaining masala mixture, green peas and salt. Add the cooked vegetables and mix well.

★ Serve hot with kadhi.

CHITRANA RICE

A highly spiced South Indian rice.
Preparation time: 20 minutes · Cooking time: 10 minutes · Serves 6 to 8.

1½ teacups uncooked rice
3 tablespoons peanuts
3 tablespoons sesame seeds
1 tablespoon gram dal
3 red chillies
5 curry leaves
½ teaspoon mustard seeds
¼ teaspoon asafoetida
2 tablespoons grated coconut
3 tablespoons tamarind water
2 tablespoons malagapadi powder
¼ teaspoon turmeric powder
2 tablespoons ghee
salt to taste

1. Boil the rice. Each grain of the cooked rice should be separate. Drain and cool.
2. Roast the peanuts and sesame seeds separately and powder them coarsely.
3. Heat the ghee, add the gram dal and mustard seeds and roast for 1 minute.
4. Add the red chillies, curry leaves and asafoetida and cook again for ½ minute.
5. Finally, add the rice, coconut, tamarind water, turmeric powder, malagapadi powder, roasted peanuts, sesame seeds and salt and cook for a few minutes.

★ Serve hot.

For the malagapadi powder

2 tablespoons coriander seeds
1½ tablespoons cumin seeds
2 tablespoons gram dal
2 tablespoons urad dal
2 tablespoons sesame seeds (til seeds)
12 red chillies
1 teaspoon asafoetida
1 teaspoon salt

For the malagapadi powder

Mix and roast all the ingredients. When roasted, powder and store in an airtight vessel.

BAKED GOAN CURRY WITH RICE PICTURE ON FACING PAGE

Do try this tasty rice and curry combination.
Preparation time: 20 minutes · Cooking time: 30 minutes · Serves 6 to 8.

For the rice
2 teacups uncooked rice
1 large coconut
2 sticks cinnamon
2 cloves
2 sliced onions
2 tablespoons ghee
salt to taste

For the paste
1 large onion, sliced
½ grated coconut
1 tablespoon coriander seeds
1½ teaspoons cumin seeds
3 sticks cinnamon
3 cloves
3 peppercorns
5 cloves garlic
10 to 12 Kashmiri chillies
1 tablespoon khus-khus
1 teaspoon oil

For the curry
3 teacups mixed boiled
   vegetables (french beans,
   carrots, cauliflower, green
   peas, potatoes)
2 large tomatoes
1 tablespoon fresh cream
½ teaspoon sugar
3 tablespoons ghee
salt to taste

For decoration
fried onions
fried cashewnuts

For the rice
1. Grate the coconut, add 3½ teacups of water
   and allow to stand for a little while. Blend in a
   liquidiser and strain.
2. Heat the ghee and fry the onions for 1 minute.
3. Add the cinnamons and cloves and fry again
   for a little while.
4. Add the rice, coconut milk and salt.
5. Cover and cook until the rice is tender.

For the paste
1. Heat the oil and fry the remaining ingredients
   for 1½ minutes.
2. Grind into a paste with the help of water.

For the curry
1. Put the tomatoes in hot water for 10 minutes.
   Grate into a pulp.
2. Heat the ghee and fry the paste for 1 minute.
3. Add the vegetables, grated tomatoes and
   ½ teacup of water and boil for 3 to 4 minutes.
4. Add the cream, sugar and salt.

How to serve
In a large baking tray, spread the curry, then
cover with the rice. Top with the fried onions
and cashewnuts and cover the tray with
aluminium foil. Bake in a hot oven at 450°F for
25 minutes.

★ Serve hot.

FACING PAGE
1 BAKED GOAN CURRY WITH RICE
2 RASGULLA DELIGHT

NAVRATNA PULLAV

A Moghlai rice, delicately spiced.
Preparation time: 15 minutes · Cooking time: 25 minutes · Serves 6 to 8.

2 teacups uncooked rice
1 tablespoon cashewnuts
1 tablespoon raisins
2 sliced onions
2 tablespoons paneer (cut into small cubes)
1 teacup boiled green peas
½ teacup boiled and diced carrots
1 teaspoon shah-jira
2 sticks cinnamon
2 cloves
3 cardamoms
1 tablespoon fruit pieces (any stewed fruit)
¼ teaspoon saffron
4 tablespoons ghee
salt to taste
onion roses for decoration

To be ground into a paste
4 cloves garlic
25 mm. (1″) piece ginger
4 green chillies

1. Boil the rice. Each grain of the cooked rice should be separate. Drain and cool.
2. Heat the ghee and fry the cashewnuts. Remove and keep aside.
3. Fry the raisins in the same ghee. Remove and keep aside.
4. Fry the onions in the same ghee till golden in colour. Remove and keep aside.
5. Add the shah-jira, cinnamon, cloves and cardamoms to the ghee and fry again.
6. Add the rice, paneer, green peas, carrots, fruit pieces, paste and salt and mix well.
7. Warm the saffron a little, rub in a little warm water and add to the rice.
8. Decorate with the fried cashewnuts, raisins, onions and onion flowers.

★ Serve hot with spicy green curds (fresh curds mixed with green chutney).

FACING PAGE
1 VEGETABLE FLORENTINE
2 ORANGE AND LEMON CREAM
3 MILANAISE SOUP
4 JIFFY FRUIT AND VEGETABLE SALAD

BAKED BAJRA ROTI

A healthy breakfast dish.
Preparation time: 15 minutes · Cooking time: 15 minutes · Makes about 4 rotis.

For the rotis
2 teacups bajra flour
1 tablespoon oil
a pinch salt

For the topping
1 teacup crumbled paneer
2 tablespoons chopped
   fenugreek leaves (methi bhaji)
1 chopped green chilli
1 finely chopped large tomato
salt to taste

For baking
a little melted unsalted butter

For the rotis
1. Mix the ingredients for the rotis and make a soft dough by adding warm water.
2. Knead the dough for 1 minute.
3. Roll out round chapatis about 100 mm. (4″) in diameter.
4. Arrange the rotis on a large greased baking tray. Bake in a hot oven at 400°F for 10 minutes.

For the topping
1. Mix the ingredients for the topping and spread over the baked rotis.
2. Trickle melted butter all over and bake in a hot oven at 400°F for 5 minutes.

★ Serve hot.

RASGULLA DELIGHT PICTURE ON PAGE 63

A very special way of serving rasgullas.
Preparation time: 15 minutes · No cooking · Makes 24 pieces.

12 rasgullas
400 grams (14 oz.) paneer
¾ teacup powdered sugar
4 powdered cardamoms
¼ teaspoon saffron
a few drops green colouring
fresh cream and fruit for
   decoration

1. Warm the saffron in a small vessel, add a little milk and rub until the saffron dissolves.
2. Grind the paneer, sugar and saffron together.
3. Add the cardamom powder and mix well.
4. Drain the rasgullas thoroughly and squeeze out a little water.
5. Take a little portion of the ground paneer and cover each rasgulla with it. Chill for ½ hour.
6. Cut each rasgulla into two parts.
7. To the remaining paneer mixture, add a few drops of green colouring. Make small balls and put on top of the cut rasgullas. Alternatively, pipe a little cream on top and decorate with cherries.

★ Put in paper cups and serve.

MALAI LADDOOS

Light, non-traditional laddoos.
Preparation time: 5 minutes · Cooking time: 20 to 30 minutes · Makes 8 to 10 small laddoos.

1½ litres (2⅝ pints) milk
100 grams (3½ oz.) castor sugar
2 small pieces alum (not more than 2 pinches)

1. Put the milk to boil.
2. After it starts boiling, add the alum.
3. Heat on a high flame and go on stirring until it is quite thick.
4. Cool.
5. Add the sugar and mix well.
6. Shape into round balls (laddoos) of the desired size.

   ★ Put in paper cups and serve.

   Note: If you like, add cut dry fruit at step 5. Alternatively, you can add a little saffron (dissolved in warm milk or water) at step 5 and serve decorated with sliced blanched almonds and pistachios.

MISRI MAWA

A quick and tasty mawa.
Preparation time: 5 minutes · Cooking time: 15 minutes · Makes 10 to 12 pieces.

1 litre (1¾ pints) milk
100 grams (3½ oz.) sugar
2 tablespoons fresh curds
⅛ teaspoon saffron
½ teaspoon cardamom powder
a few chopped blanched almonds and pistachios for decoration

1. Mix the milk, sugar and curds. Boil on a high flame.
2. Go on cooking and stirring until the mixture is fairly thick.
3. Prepare the saffron by rubbing in a little warm milk or water.
4. Add the saffron liquid and cardamom powder to the mixture. Mix well.
5. Spread the mixture on a plate. Cool.
6. Chill for at least 2 hours.
7. Decorate with almonds and pistachios.

   ★ Cut into pieces and serve.

MILK CAKE

A wholesome sweet.
Preparation time: 5 minutes · Cooking time: 20 to 30 minutes · Makes 8 to 10 pieces.

1½ litres (2⅝ pints) milk
100 grams (3½ oz.) sugar
2 small pieces alum (not more than 2 pinches)

1. Put the milk to boil.
2. After it starts boiling, add the alum.
3. Heat on a high flame and go on stirring until it becomes half in quantity.
4. Add the sugar and go on cooking until quite thick.
5. Spread the mixture on to a well-greased plate and allow to cool for at least 6 to 7 hours.
6. Store in the refrigerator.

★ Cut into pieces and serve.

MILK AND NUT BARFI

A delicious barfi, flavoured with saffron.
Preparation time: 5 minutes · Cooking time: 20 to 30 minutes · Makes 12 pieces.

1 litre (1¾ pints) milk
100 grams (3½ oz.) sugar
2 small pieces alum (not more than 2 pinches)
¼ teaspoon saffron
50 grams (2 oz.) coarsely powdered almonds or cashewnuts
¼ teaspoon cardamom powder

1. Put the milk to boil.
2. After it starts boiling, add the alum.
3. Heat on a high flame and go on stirring until it becomes half in quantity.
4. Add the sugar and go on cooking until quite thick.
5. Warm the saffron and rub into a little water. Add to the mixture.
6. Add the almonds and cardamom and cook for ½ minute.
7. Spread the mixture on to a well-greased plate and allow to cool for 6 hours.

★ Cut into pieces and serve.

VI. Western Style Main Dishes

VEGETABLE FLORENTINE PICTURE ON PAGE 64

A superb spinach dish without eggs.
Preparation time: 10 minutes · Cooking time: 40 minutes · Serves 6 to 8.

For the spinach
5 bundles spinach
1 chopped onion
2 teaspoons plain flour
   (optional)
2 chopped green chillies
a pinch soda bi-carb
2 tablespoons fresh cream
1 tablespoon ghee
salt and pepper to taste

For the vegetables
3 teacups mixed boiled
   vegetables (french beans,
   carrots, green peas)
3 teacups white sauce, *page 164*
¾ teacup thick curds (optional)
2 tablespoons grated cooking
   cheese
salt and pepper to taste

For baking
2 tablespoons grated cooking
   cheese

For the spinach
1. Chop the spinach very finely. Add the soda
   bi-carb and 2 tablespoons of water.
2. Cook until soft, then drain the liquid.
3. Blend in a liquidiser.
4. Heat the ghee and fry the onion, flour and
   green chillies for ½ minute.
5. Add the spinach, cream, salt and pepper.
   Cook for 1 minute.

For the vegetables
   Mix all the ingredients.

How to proceed
1. Spread the spinach mixture on a greased
   baking dish and cover with the vegetable
   mixture.
2. Sprinkle the cooking cheese and bake in a hot
   oven at 450°F for about 20 minutes.

   ★ Serve hot.

69

CHEESY BAKED RICE WITH VEGETABLES

A tasty and economical dish suitable for lunch and dinner.
Preparation time: 20 minutes · Cooking time: 30 minutes · Serves 6 to 8.

For the rice
2 teacups cooked rice
1 tablespoon butter
½ teacup milk
salt to taste

For the sauce
3 teacups milk
1½ teacups water
1 chopped onion
3 tablespoons butter
3 tablespoons plain flour
2 chopped green chillies
2 tablespoons grated cheese
salt to taste

Other ingredients
2 teacups mixed boiled
   vegetables (french beans,
   carrots, cauliflower, green
   peas)
4 tablespoons grated cheese

For the rice
   Heat the butter. Add the rice, milk and salt and
   cook for a few minutes.

For the sauce
1. Heat the butter and fry the onion for 1 minute.
2. Add the plain flour and green chillies. Fry for a
   few minutes.
3. Add the milk, water and salt. Go on stirring
   until the mixture becomes thick.
4. Add the cheese.

How to proceed
1. Add 2 teacups of the sauce to the vegetables
   and mix well.
2. Spread a little of the balance sauce on a
   greased baking dish. Spread all the rice, and
   then the remaining sauce.
3. Cover with the cheese and bake in a hot oven
   at 450°F for 20 minutes.

   ★ Serve hot.

BAKED CORN SANDWICHES

A superb party dish.
Preparation time: 10 minutes · Cooking time: 30 minutes · Serves 6 to 8.

1 loaf sliced bread
1 packet frozen corn *or*
  2 teacups cooked corn
1 chopped onion
2 chopped green chillies
1 tablespoon ghee *or* butter
2 pinches sugar
1 teacup milk
2½ teacups white sauce,
  page 164
4 tablespoons grated cooking
  cheese
salt and pepper to taste

1. Heat the ghee and fry the onion for 1 minute. Add the chillies and fry again for a few seconds.
2. Add the corn, sugar and salt and ½ teacup of the white sauce.
3. Remove the crust from the bread slices.
4. Cut into triangles.
5. Dip the bread triangles in the milk. Make sandwiches with the corn mixture.
6. Arrange the sandwiches on a greased baking tray. Put 2 pinches of salt in the remaining milk and pour on top.
7. Add salt, pepper and half of the cheese to the remaining white sauce. Spread over the sandwiches. Sprinkle the remaining cheese on top.
8. Bake in a hot oven at 450°F for 20 minutes.

★ Serve hot.

Note: There is another way of making this dish. Instead of making sandwiches, make firstly a layer of bread slices dipped in milk, then put all the corn, a little spiced white sauce, next the remaining bread slices and finally the remaining spiced white sauce and cheese. Bake in the same manner.

STUFFED POTATOES WITH CORN PICTURE ON PAGE 35

A simple dish enlivened by an unusual sauce.
Preparation time: 20 minutes · Cooking time: 40 to 50 minutes · Serves 6 to 8.

12 medium sized potatoes (old)
2 teacups cooked corn
1 chopped onion
2 chopped green chillies
2 tablespoons butter
½ teacup milk
2 tablespoons fresh cream
2 level teaspoons plain flour
salt to taste

For the sauce
2 large tomatoes
1 teacup fresh cream
1 teacup milk
4 tablespoons tomato ketchup
1 tablespoon plain flour
½ teaspoon chilli powder
2 teaspoons sugar (approx.)
salt to taste

For baking
2 tablespoons grated cooking
    cheese

1. Boil the potatoes with the skins on.
2. Remove the skins and cut each potato into two equal parts.
3. Scoop out the centres.
4. Heat the butter and fry the onion for 1 minute.
5. Add the green chillies and fry again for a few seconds. Add the corn.
6. Mix the milk, cream and flour and add to the corn mixture. Add salt and mix. Cook for a few minutes.
7. Stuff the potatoes with the corn mixture.

For the sauce
1. Cut the tomatoes into big pieces, add ¼ teacup of water and cook. When cooked, take out a thick soup by passing through a sieve.
2. Add the cream, milk, tomato ketchup, flour and 1 teacup of water.
3. Add the chilli powder, sugar and salt. Boil until thick.

How to proceed
Arrange the potatoes on a baking dish, pour the sauce and sprinkle the cheese on top.
Bake in a hot oven at 450°F for 15 to 20 minutes.

★ Serve hot.

BAKED LASAGNA WITH VEGETABLES

A vegetarian version of the famous Italian dish.
Preparation time: 20 minutes · Cooking time: 40 minutes · Serves 6 to 8.

For the lasagna

2 teacups plain flour
2 tablespoons butter
1 teacup chopped spinach
½ teaspoon salt

for the stuffing
3 teacups mixed boiled
vegetables (french beans,
carrots, green peas)
2 boiled potatoes
chopped onion
chopped green chillies
pinches garam masala
(optional)
tablespoon ghee
salt to taste

For the topping
teacups white sauce page 164
4 tablespoons grated cooking
cheese
a little butter

For the lasagna

1. Blend the spinach in a liquidiser with 2 tablespoons of water.
2. Apply butter to the flour and add salt.
3. Add the spinach liquid and make a soft dough.
4. Roll out the dough into big thin chapatis with the help of a little flour. Cut into broad strips.
5. Boil plenty of water in a big vessel. Add 1 tablespoon of oil to the boiling water.
6. Cook a few strips at a time in the boiling water and remove after ½ minute.

For the stuffing

1. Mash the potatoes coarsely.
2. Heat the ghee and fry the onion for 1 minute.
3. Add all the remaining ingredients.

How to proceed

1. In a greased baking dish, pour a little white sauce and arrange some of the lasagna strips over the sauce.
2. Sprinkle half of the stuffing over the strips.
3. Pour a little white sauce again.
4. Again arrange some strips over the sauce.
5. Sprinkle the balance stuffing over the strips.
6. Arrange the remaining strips on top.
7. Sprinkle the cheese on top and dot with butter.
8. Bake in a hot oven at 450°F for 20 to 25 minutes or until golden brown.

★ Serve hot.

Note: The above simplified recipe for lasagna should be used where ready-made lasagna is not available in the market.

RICE AND SPAGHETTI BALLS IN TOMATO GRAVY

A dish which never fails to please.
Preparation time: 20 minutes · Cooking time: 40 minutes · Serves 6 to 8.

For the balls
1½ teacups cooked rice
1½ teacups cooked spaghetti
2 tablespoons chopped
   coriander
3 to 4 chopped green chillies
4 tablespoons butter
5 tablespoons plain flour
1½ teacups milk
salt to taste
½ teacup plain flour mixed with
   1 teacup water and a pinch
   salt
bread crumbs
oil for deep frying

For the tomato gravy
1½ kg. (3⅜ lb.) big red
   tomatoes
4 teaspoons sugar (approx.)
3 to 4 tablespoons fresh cream
1 teaspoon chilli powder
3 to 4 tablespoons baked beans
   in tomato gravy (optional)
salt to taste

For serving
2 tablespoons grated cheese
potato wafers

For the balls
1. Heat the butter and fry the flour for 1 minute.
2. Add the milk and beat.
3. Cook until the sauce is very thick.
4. Cool the sauce.
5. Add the rice, spaghetti, coriander, green chillies and salt. Mix and shape into balls.
6. Make a batter by mixing the flour, water and salt.
7. Dip the balls in this batter, roll into bread crumbs and deep fry in oil until crisp.

For the tomato gravy
1. Cut the tomatoes into big pieces, add 1 tablespoon of water and cook. When cooked, prepare a thick soup by passing through a sieve.
2. Add the sugar, salt and chilli powder and boil for at least 10 minutes.
3. Add the baked beans and cream.

How to serve
Put the balls in a serving tray and pour the gravy on top. Sprinkle cheese and surround with potato wafers.

★ Serve hot.

POTATO RING WITH SPAGHETTI IN TOMATO SAUCE

A two-in-one dish.
Preparation time: 10 minutes · Cooking time: 40 minutes · Serves 6 to 8.

For the potato ring
4 boiled potatoes
3 chopped green chillies
1 teacup cooked corn
½ teacup cooked spaghetti
½ teacup milk
1 chopped onion
1 tablespoon butter
salt to taste

For the spaghetti in tomato sauce
1 kg. (2¼ lb.) tomatoes
3 teacups boiled spaghetti
1 chopped onion
½ teaspoon chilli powder
3 teaspoons sugar (approx.)
3 tablespoons fresh cream
2 tablespoons ghee
salt to taste

To serve
grated cheese

For the potato ring
1. Cut the potatoes into small pieces.
2. Heat the butter and fry the onion for 1 minute. Add the chillies and fry again for a few seconds.
3. Add the potatoes, corn, spaghetti, milk and salt. Keep the mixture hot.

For the spaghetti in tomato sauce
1. Cut the tomatoes into big pieces, add 2 tablespoons of water and cook. When cooked, take out a thick soup by passing through a sieve.
2. Heat the ghee and fry the onion for 1 minute.
3. Add the tomato soup, chilli powder, sugar and salt and boil for about 10 minutes.
4. Add the spaghetti and cream.

How to serve
Fill the hot potato mixture into a ring mould (or in any jelly mould). Invert on a serving dish. Surround with the spaghetti in tomato sauce. Sprinkle grated cheese on top.

★ Serve hot.

STACKED PANCAKES PICTURE ON PAGE 36

A mouth-watering main dish.
Preparation time: 20 minutes · Cooking time: 40 minutes · Serves 6 to 8.

For the pancakes
175 grams (6 oz.) plain flour
300 ml. (10 fl. oz.) milk
4 teaspoons melted butter
½ teaspoon baking powder
½ teaspoon salt
ghee *or* butter for frying

For the filling
2 teacups mixed boiled
   vegetables (french beans,
   carrots, green peas)
2 large boiled potatoes
1 chopped onion
1 tablespoon chopped
   coriander
2 chopped green chillies
1 teaspoon chilli powder
2 tablespoons ghee
salt to taste

For the sauce
1 kg. (2¼ lb.) red tomatoes
100 grams (4 oz.) fresh cream
½ teaspoon chilli powder
2 teaspoons sugar
salt to taste

To serve
grated cheese and potato
   wafers

For the pancakes
1. Mix all the ingredients together. Leave the batter for 20 minutes.
2. Prepare pancakes of about 150 mm. (6") diameter in a non-stick frying pan using a little ghee or butter.

For the filling
1. Mash the potatoes coarsely.
2. Heat the ghee and fry the onion for 1 minute.
3. Add the remaining ingredients, mix well and cook for a few minutes.

For the sauce
1. Cut the tomatoes into big pieces, add 1 tablespoon of water and cook. When cooked, take out a thick soup by passing through a sieve.
2. Add the chilli powder, sugar and salt and boil for 10 minutes.
3. Add the cream. Mix well.

How to proceed
1. Grease a baking dish and spread a little sauce at the bottom. Put a pancake over it and spread a little filling and a little sauce.
2. Repeat and build up layers of pancakes, filling and sauce.
3. Bake in a hot oven at 450°F for 10 to 15 minutes until cooked.

★ Sprinkle grated cheese on top and surround with potato wafers. Serve hot.

BAKED STUFFED POTATOES

Different and delightful.
Preparation time: 20 minutes · Cooking time: 50 minutes · Serves 6 to 8.

12 medium potatoes (old)
1½ teacups mixed boiled
 vegetables (carrots, french
 beans, green peas)
1 chopped onion
1 teaspoon chilli powder
1 teaspoon soya sauce
3 teacups white sauce, *page 164*
1 teacup thick curds
6 tablespoons grated cooking
 cheese
a little butter
2 tablespoons oil
salt and pepper to taste

1. Boil the potatoes with the skins on.
2. Remove the skins and cut each potato into
 2 equal parts.
3. Scoop out the centres.
4. Heat the oil and fry the onion for a little time.
5. Add the vegetables, scooped portion of
 potatoes, chilli powder, soya sauce and salt
 and cook for 1 minute.
6. Fill the potatoes with the stuffing.
7. Add salt, pepper, the curds and half of the
 cheese to the white sauce.
8. Arrange the potatoes in a baking dish, cover
 with this sauce and the remaining cheese.
9. Dot with butter and bake in a hot oven at 450°F
 for 25 minutes.

★ Serve immediately.

MACARONI SUPREME

A macaroni and parsley combination.
Preparation time: 15 minutes · Cooking time: 30 minutes · Serves 6 to 8.

3 teacups boiled macaroni
3½ teacups white sauce,
 page 164
½ teacup chopped parsley
¼ teaspoon nutmeg powder
½ teaspoon dried *or* fresh
 oregano
1 teacup grated cheese
1 sliced tomato
a little butter
salt and pepper to taste

1. Add the parsley, nutmeg powder, oregano,
 salt and pepper and three-quarters of the
 cheese to the white sauce.
2. Mix the macaroni and white sauce and spread
 on a greased baking dish. Put the tomato slices
 on top.
3. Cover with the remaining cheese and dot with
 butter. Bake in a hot oven at 450°F for about
 25 minutes.

★ Serve hot.

CHINESE STYLE BAKED PANCAKES

Chinese ingredients lend a special touch to ordinary pancakes.
Preparation time: 20 minutes · Cooking time: 40 minutes · Serves 6 to 8.

For the pancakes
100 grams (4 oz.) plain flour
300 ml. (10 fl. oz.) milk
3 teaspoons ghee
a pinch salt

For the stuffing
1 teacup boiled noodles
2 teacups shredded cabbage
1 sliced capsicum
2 sliced onions
2 grated carrots
1 teacup bean sprouts
2 to 3 tablespoons sliced
    mushrooms (optional)
¼ teaspoon Ajinomoto powder
¼ teaspoon chilli powder
½ teaspoon soya sauce
2 tablespoons oil
salt to taste

For the tomato gravy
4 tomatoes
½ teaspoon chilli powder
1½ teaspoons sugar
2 tablespoons fresh cream
salt to taste

To be mixed into a sauce
2 teacups white sauce, *page 164*
2 tablespoons grated cheese
2 tablespoons thick curds
salt and pepper to taste

For baking
2 tablespoons grated cheese

For the pancakes
Mix all the ingredients into a batter. Make thin pancakes in a non-stick frying pan with the help of little ghee.

For the stuffing
1. Heat the oil on a high flame. Add the vegetables and Ajinomoto powder and cook for 3 to 4 minutes.
2. Add the noodles, chilli powder, soya sauce and salt and cook for 1 minute.

For the tomato gravy
1. Cut the tomatoes into big pieces, add 1 tablespoon of water and cook. When cooked, take out soup through a sieve.
2. Add the chilli powder, sugar and salt and boil for 10 minutes.
3. Add the cream.

How to proceed
1. Spread the white sauce in a baking dish. Then put a pancake, a little stuffing and some tomato gravy. Build up layers in this manner.
2. Cover with the balance white sauce and the grated cheese. Bake in a hot oven at 450°F for 20 minutes.

★ Serve hot.

CANNELONI FROM EAST AND WEST

Indian paneer with fruit and cheese makes this canneloni dish unusual and exciting.
Preparation time: 20 minutes · Cooking time: 30 minutes · Serves 6 to 8.

For the dough
1½ teacups plain flour
3 teaspoons oil
½ teaspoon salt

For the stuffing
1 small can (450 grams) pineapple slices
200 grams (7 oz.) finely chopped paneer
1 chopped onion
2 chopped green chillies
2 tablespoons grated cooking cheese
1 tablespoon ghee
salt to taste

For the sauce
1 kg. (2¼ lb.) tomatoes
2 chopped onions
3 cloves crushed garlic
1½ teaspoons sugar (approx.)
1½ teaspoons chilli powder
1 tablespoon oil
salt to taste

For baking
1 teacup white sauce, *page 164*
4 tablespoons grated cheese

For the dough
Mix all the ingredients and make a soft dough by adding water. Knead well.

For the stuffing
1. Drain the pineapple slices and chop finely.
2. Heat the ghee and fry the onion for 1 minute.
3. Add the green chillies and fry again for a few seconds.
4. Add the paneer, cheese, pineapple and salt.

For the sauce
1. Chop the tomatoes.
2. Heat the oil and fry the onions and garlic for ½ minute.
3. Add the tomatoes and cook for 10 minutes at least.
4. Blend the mixture in a liquidiser.
5. Add the sugar, chilli powder and salt and boil again for a few minutes.

How to proceed
1. Put plenty of water to boil. Add 1 tablespoon of oil to the boiling water.
2. Roll out small thin chapatis from the dough and cook one at a time in the boiling water.
3. Spread a little stuffing on a cooked chapati and fold. Repeat for the remaining chapatis and stuffing.
4. Pour a little sauce on the base of a baking tray. Arrange the canneloni over it and pour the remaining sauce on top.
5. Spread the white sauce over it and sprinkle the cheese on top.
6. Bake in a hot oven at 450°F for 20 to 25 minutes.

   ★ Serve hot.

EGGPLANT PARMESAN PICTURE ON FACING PAGE

A popular dish.
Preparation time: 20 minutes · Cooking time: 30 minutes · Serves 6 to 8.

2 eggplants
2 potatoes
5 to 6 tablespoons cooking
   cheese
1 teacup white sauce, *page 164*
oil for deep frying

For the tomato sauce
1 kg. (2¼ lb.) large tomatoes
1 large chopped onion
4 cloves crushed garlic
8 finely chopped basil leaves
   or tulsi paan
2 pinches ajwain
½ teaspoon chilli powder
½ teaspoon sugar
2 tablespoons oil
salt to taste

1. Slice the eggplants and potatoes.
2. Deep fry in oil.

For the tomato sauce
1. Heat the oil and fry the onion for 2 to 3
   minutes.
2. Add the tomatoes, garlic, basil leaves, ajwain,
   chilli powder, sugar and salt and boil for 10
   minutes.
3. Beat the sauce.

How to proceed
Spread a little sauce on the bottom of a
greased baking dish. Put a few eggplants and
potato slices on it and sprinkle a little cheese
and white sauce on top. Make more layers in
this manner. Finally spread the white sauce
and top with cheese. Bake at 400°F in a hot
oven for 15 minutes.

★ Serve hot.

Variation: SPAGHETTI AND RAJMA PARMESAN Use 1 teacup boiled
spaghetti (or macaroni) and 1 teacup cooked rajma in place of the eggplants and
potatoes.

FACING PAGE
1 NOUGAT CAKE
2 BREAD AND BEAN SALAD
3 SPICY BEAN AND TOMATO SOUP
4 EGGPLANT PARMESAN

SPINACH AND BEAN PIZZA PICTURE ON FACING PAGE

A colourful and tasty pizza.
Preparation time: 40 minutes · Cooking time: 40 minutes · Makes 10 to 12 small pizzas.

For the dough
500 grams (1⅛ lb.) plain flour
20 grams (¾ oz.) fresh yeast
1 teaspoon sugar
4 teaspoons oil
1 teaspoon salt

For the spinach topping
5 bundles spinach
2 tablespoons white sauce, *page 164*
1 chopped onion
2 to 3 chopped green chillies
2 pinches soda bi-carb
1 tablespoon ghee
salt and pepper to taste

For the bean topping
1 small can (225 grams) baked beans
1 chopped onion
2 to 3 chopped green chillies
1 tablespoon ghee

For cooking
1 teacup white sauce, *page 164*
5 to 6 tablespoons grated cheese

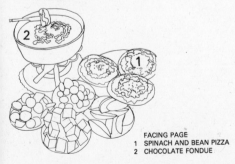

FACING PAGE
1 SPINACH AND BEAN PIZZA
2 CHOCOLATE FONDUE

For the dough
1. Sieve the flour. Make a well in the centre, add the fresh yeast, sugar and about ½ teacup of warm water and dissolve the yeast in the water.
2. After 2 minutes, mix the flour and yeast and add enough warm water to make a soft dough.
3. Knead the dough for 4 to 5 minutes. Mix the oil and salt, add to the dough and knead again for ½ minute.
4. Cover the dough with cloth and allow to rest for 25 minutes or until double in size.

For the spinach topping
1. Chop the spinach very finely.
2. Boil plenty of water. Add the soda bi-carb and spinach and cook for a few minutes. Drain.
3. Heat the ghee and fry the onion and chillies for 1 minute.
4. Add the spinach, white sauce, salt and pepper and cook for 1 minute.

For the bean topping
1. Heat the ghee and fry the onion and chillies for 1 minute.
2. Add the baked beans and mix well.

How to proceed
1. Knead the dough and divide into 10 to 12 parts.
2. Shape the portions into small balls and press flat with the help of a flat surface e.g. glass bottom.
3. Wait for 15 to 20 minutes.
4. Spread a little spinach and baked beans, cover with white sauce and sprinkle grated cheese.
5. Bake in a hot oven at 450°F for 20 to 25 minutes.

★ Serve hot.

Variation 1: **SPINACH AND MUSHROOM PIZZA** Substitute the baked beans by the same quantity of cooked and chopped mushrooms and add salt to taste.

Variation 2: **BEAN PIZZA** Omit the spinach mixture and use double the ingredients for the bean topping.

BAKED MACARONI WITH VEGETABLES

A simple but delightful combination of macaroni and vegetables with a dash of chillies.
Preparation time: 15 minutes · Cooking time: 25 minutes · Serves 6 to 8.

2 teacups boiled macaroni
(cut macaroni)
1½ teacups shredded cabbage
1½ teacups chopped spinach
3 chopped green chillies
1 chopped onion
2 tablespoons ghee
a pinch Ajinomoto powder
2 teacups white sauce, *page 164*
4 tablespoons grated cooking
cheese
a little butter
salt and pepper to taste

1. Heat the ghee and fry the onion for 1 minute. Add the chillies and fry again for a few seconds.
2. Add the cabbage, spinach and Ajinomoto powder and fry again for 2 to 3 minutes.
3. Add the macaroni and salt and mix well.
4. Spread the mixture in a greased baking dish.
5. Add half the cheese to the white sauce. Add salt and pepper and mix well.
6. Just before serving, spread this sauce over the macaroni mixture. Sprinkle the remaining cheese, dot with butter and bake in a hot oven at 450°F for 20 minutes or until golden brown.

★ Serve hot.

VII. Ice-Creams

CHOCONUT ICE-CREAM

Rich, crunchy and tasty.
Preparation time: 10 minutes · Cooking time: 30 minutes · Serves 10.

8 teacups milk
3 teacups fresh cream
4 tablespoons cocoa
1½ teacups powdered sugar
2 teaspoons vanilla essence
4 teaspoons Bournvita
2 level tablespoons cornflour
1 recipe praline powder,
   page 166

1. Mix the cornflour and cocoa in 2 teacups of cold milk. Put to boil and go on stirring until the mixture becomes thick. Cool.
2. Beat the cream with half the sugar until thick.
3. Mix the remaining milk and sugar with the cocoa mixture, beaten cream, vanilla essence and Bournvita.
4. Add the praline powder to the milk mixture.
5. Prepare the ice-cream in an ice-cream churner.

★ Serve.

CHOCOLATE VELVET ICE-CREAM

An evening ice-cream for a small family.
Preparation time: 10 minutes · Cooking time: 10 minutes · Serves 5 to 6.

600 ml. (20 fl. oz.) milk
2 level tablespoons cornflour
1 level tablespoon cocoa
200 to 300 grams (7 to 10 oz.)
   fresh cream
6 tablespoons sugar
1 teaspoon vanilla essence
3 to 4 tablespoons roasted
   almonds *or* chopped walnuts

1. Beat the cream lightly.
2. Mix the cornflour and cocoa in ¾ teacup of cold milk.
3. Mix the remaining milk, cocoa mixture, cream and sugar and boil until the mixture becomes thick.
4. Cool and add the vanilla essence.
5. Pour into ice trays and put to set in the freezer compartment of a refrigerator directly over the freezing plate.
6. When almost set, remove the frozen mixture into a chilled bowl and beat with a fork.
7. Put to set again as above.
8. When set, beat once again with a fork.
9. Put to set for a third time in the same manner.
10. Before serving, remove at least 10 minutes in advance from the freezer.

★ Serve in individual cups after sprinkling nuts.

CHOCOLATE AND STRAWBERRY SUNDAE

PICTURE ON PAGE 100

This combination of ice-cream, jelly and strawberry sauce is a sure winner with children.

Preparation time: 30 minutes · Cooking time: 20 minutes · Serves 10.

For the ice-cream
1½ litres (2⅝ pints) milk
500 grams (1⅛ lb.) fresh cream
1½ teacups powdered sugar
    (approx.)
2 teaspoons vanilla essence
3 level tablespoons cornflour

For the strawberry sauce
1 small can (450 grams)
    strawberries
2 level teaspoons cornflour
1 tablespoon sugar
a few drops lemon juice
a few drops red colouring

For the jelly
½ packet (of a 100 grams full
    packet) strawberry jelly

For serving
grated chocolate and wafer
    biscuits

For the ice-cream
1. Mix ½ litre of milk with the cornflour very well.
2. Put to boil on a medium flame.
3. Go on stirring until the mixture becomes thick. Then add the remaining 1 litre milk and mix.
4. Beat the cream and three-quarters of the sugar until thick.
5. Mix the milk, cream, the remaining sugar and the vanilla essence. Taste and add sugar if required.

For the strawberry sauce
1. Take out syrup from the strawberry can and add the cornflour and sugar.
2. Put to boil and go on stirring until the mixture gets thicker. Take off the fire and cool.
3. Add the strawberries, lemon juice and colouring.

For the jelly
Dissolve the jelly in 1½ teacups of boiling water. Cool and put to set in the refrigerator.

How to serve
In a tall glass, put a little jelly at the bottom. Then make layers of ice-cream and strawberry sauce. Finally, sprinkle a little grated chocolate and put a wafer biscuit on top. Fill other sundae glasses similarly.

★ Serve cold.

Note: You can also use ready-made vanilla ice-cream if short of time.

CHOCOMINT ICE-CREAM

For the mint and chocolate lovers.
Preparation time: 10 minutes · Cooking time: 30 minutes · Serves 12.

1½ litres (2⅝ pints) milk
1 kg. (2¼ lb.) fresh cream
3 level tablespoons cornflour
1½ teacups powdered sugar
  (approx.)
2 teaspoons peppermint
  essence (approx.)
1 teacup milk chocolate cut into
  pieces
a few drops of green colouring

1. Add the cornflour to half of the cold milk. Put to boil and go on stirring until the mixture becomes thick. Add the rest of the milk and mix very well.
2. Beat the cream with the sugar until thick and fluffy.
3. Add the milk, peppermint essence and chocolate pieces and mix well.
4. Prepare the ice-cream in an ice-cream churner or in a refrigerator.

   ★ Serve.

   Note: This ice-cream is extremely rich. To make it less rich, reduce the quantity of cream to half.

VANILLA ICE-CREAM WITH MINT PINEAPPLE SAUCE

Do not prepare this minty sauce without creme de menthe.
Preparation time: 10 minutes · Cooking time: 20 minutes · Serves 10.

2 level tablespoons cornflour
2 litres (3½ pints) milk
1 kg. (2¼ lb.) fresh cream
1½ teacups powdered sugar
2 teaspoons vanilla essence

1. Mix the cornflour and ½ litre of milk.
2. Boil the mixture and go on stirring until it is thick.
3. Beat the cream with half of the sugar.
4. Mix the cornflour mixture, beaten cream, vanilla essence and the remaining milk and sugar.
5. Prepare the ice-cream in an ice-cream churner.

   ★ Serve with the mint pineapple sauce.

For the mint pineapple sauce
1 small can (450 grams)
  pineapple slices
2 level teaspoons cornflour
2 tablespoons sugar
1 tablespoon lemon juice
½ teaspoon peppermint
  essence
½ teacup creme de menthe

For the mint pineapple sauce
1. Chop the pineapple slices very finely. Keep aside the syrup.
2. Mix the cornflour, sugar and syrup from the can and boil until thick.
3. Add the pineapple, lemon juice, peppermint essence and creme de menthe and mix well.
4. Chill thoroughly.

87

VIII. Puddings and Pies

ICE-CREAM AND JELLY DELIGHT

Even teenagers can prepare this simple pudding.
Preparation time: a few minutes · Setting time: 20 minutes · Serves 8.

1 family pack (½ litre) vanilla
  ice-cream
1 packet (100 grams) raspberry
  jelly
sweetened cream and cherries
  for decoration

1. Dissolve the jelly in 3 teacups of boiling water.
2. Pour over the ice-cream.
3. Stir the mixture for 2 to 3 minutes over ice.
4. Pour into wettened individual moulds (or a fancy mould as desired) and put to set in the refrigerator.
5. Just before serving, dip the mould/s in hot water for a few seconds, loosen the sides and unmould on a plate.

   ★ Serve in individual glasses decorated with cream and cherries.

QUICK PUDDING

A beginner's pudding.
Preparation time: 10 minutes · Setting time: 20 minutes · Serves 6 to 8.

1 small can (450 grams) orange
  segments *or* pineapple slices
1 packet (100 grams) orange *or*
  pineapple jelly
1 family pack (½ litre) vanilla
  ice-cream
¼ teaspoon orange *or*
  pineapple essence
juice of 1 lemon
¼ teaspoon grated orange rind
whipped cream and fruit pieces
  for decoration

1. Chop the canned fruit. Keep aside the syrup.
2. Mix the syrup from the fruit can with 2 teacups of water and boil.
3. When the syrup starts boiling, add the jelly and stir well.
4. Soften the vanilla ice-cream and pour the boiling jelly mixture over it. Add the essence, lemon juice and rind, mix well and pour into a wetted mould.
5. Put to set in the freezer compartment of a refrigerator.
6. Just before serving, dip the mould in hot water for a few seconds, loosen the sides and unmould on a plate.

   ★ Decorate with whipped cream and fruit pieces and serve cold.

FRUIT AND JELLY TRIFLE

The popular trifle in a different but attractive form.
Preparation time: 15 minutes · Setting time: 25 minutes · Serves 8.

1 packet (100 grams) orange jelly
200 grams (7 oz.) fresh cream
½ slice any sponge cake
1 small can (450 grams) fruit cocktail
3 tablespoons powdered sugar
2 teaspoons orange squash
½ teaspoon lemon juice
a few drops orange essence
a few drops orange colouring
orange wafers for decoration

1. Dissolve the jelly in 2½ teacups of boiling water.
2. Cool and add the orange squash.
3. Pour a little jelly in a 175 mm. (7″) diameter sandwich cake tin and put to set in the refrigerator.
4. Drain the fruit and keep aside the syrup.
5. Beat the cream with the sugar until thick.
6. When the jelly sets, put the cake slice on top and sprinkle a little of the fruit syrup.
7. Spread the fruit pieces on top.
8. Put the vessel containing the remaining jelly mixture in a larger vessel filled with ice-cubes and go on stirring all the time.
9. When the mixture becomes slightly thick, add 1 teacup of the beaten cream and the lemon juice, orange essence and orange colouring.
10. When the mixture gets thicker, pour over the fruit and put to set in the refrigerator.
11. Just before serving, dip the mould in hot water for a few seconds and unmould on a plate.
12. Beat the remaining cream again until thick.
13. Fit a piping bag with a 12 mm. (½″) star nozzle, fill with the cream and pipe the cream around the pudding.

★ Decorate with orange wafers and serve cold.

STRAWBERRY AND PINEAPPLE SLICE

PICTURE ON PAGE 45

Colourful slices for high tea or dinner.
Preparation time: 10 minutes · Setting time: 30 minutes · Serves 6 to 8.

1 packet (100 grams) raspberry *or* strawberry jelly
1 small can (450 grams) pineapple slices
½ slice 275 mm. (9″) diameter sponge cake for puddings, *page 166*
1 teacup sliced strawberries
2 teaspoons powdered sugar
½ teaspoon lemon juice

1. Chop the pineapple slices, leaving 1 slice for decoration. Keep aside the syrup.
2. Dissolve the jelly in 2 teacups of boiling water. Cool and add 1 teacup of pineapple syrup.
3. Add the sugar and lemon juice.
4. In a round cake tin approx. 275 mm. (9″) diameter, pour ¾ teacup of the jelly and arrange the pineapple and strawberry slices decoratively. Put to set in the refrigerator.
5. Put the vessel containing the remaining jelly mixture in a larger vessel filled with ice-cubes and go on stirring all the time.
6. When the mixture is slightly thick, add the remaining fruit and mix well.
7. Pour this mixture over the set jelly.
8. Put the sponge cake slice over the jelly mixture, sprinkle a little pineapple syrup over the sponge and put to set in the refrigerator.
9. To serve, dip the mould in hot water for a few seconds, loosen the sides and unmould on a plate.

★ Cut into slices and serve.

Variation 1: PINEAPPLE AND GRAPE SLICE Use pineapple instead of raspberry jelly and fresh seedless grapes instead of pineapple slices.

Variation 2: PEACH AND PINEAPPLE SLICE Use orange instead of raspberry jelly and a small can of peaches in addition to the pineapple.

STRAWBERRY GLAZE CREAM PIE PICTURE ON PAGE 35

A spectacular party dish which is surprisingly easy to make.
Preparation time: 15 minutes · Setting time: 30 minutes · Serves 8.

For the crust
5 to 6 tablespoons coarsely
   powdered Marie biscuits
4 tablespoons melted
   margarine *or* butter
1 tablespoon powdered sugar

For the filling
½ teacup sliced strawberries
1 family pack (½ litre) vanilla
   ice-cream
1 packet (11 grams) strong
   gelatine
juice of 2 lemons
3 teaspoons sugar (granulated)
100 grams (4 oz.) fresh cream
2 tablespoons powdered sugar
½ teaspoon grated lemon rind

For the glaze
1 teacup strawberry purée
2 level teaspoons cornflour
8 teaspoons sugar
juice of ½ lemon
2 drops cochineal

For decoration
½ teacup fresh strawberries

For the crust
1. Mix the ingredients and press well into a 200
   or 225 mm. (8" or 9") diameter pie dish.
2. Either chill the crust in the freezer
   compartment of a refrigerator or bake blind in
   hot oven at 400°F for 7 to 8 minutes.

How to proceed
1. Arrange the sliced strawberries over the crust.
2. Mix the gelatine in 1 teacup of water, add the
   granulated sugar and juice of 1 lemon and
   warm on a slow flame until the gelatine
   dissolves. Pour this mixture over the
   strawberries.
3. Beat the fresh cream and the powdered sugar
   and add the remaining lemon juice.
4. Mix this cream with the ice-cream and lemon
   rind over hot water and pour the mixture over
   the strawberries.
5. Put to set in the freezer compartment of a
   refrigerator.
6. Mix the strawberry purée, cornflour and sugar
   with 1 teacup of water and boil until thick and
   clear. Cool, add the lemon juice and cochineal.
   Spread this glaze over the pie.
7. Decorate with fresh strawberries.

★ Serve chilled.

Note: You can also make this pie using
peaches or pineapple instead of strawberries.

STRAWBERRY CARNIVAL PUDDING

PICTURE ON PAGE 45

Simple to make and stunning to look at.
Preparation time: 10 minutes · Setting time: 30 minutes · Serves 6 to 8.

1 packet (100 grams) strawberry jelly
200 grams (7 oz.) fresh cream
2 tablespoons powdered sugar
¾ teacup sliced strawberries
2 small cups vanilla ice-cream
sweetened cream and fresh strawberries for decoration

1. Dissolve the jelly in 2 teacups of boiling water.
2. Cool a little and pour a small amount into a jelly mould. Put to set in the refrigerator.
3. To the remaining jelly, add the vanilla ice-cream and beat.
4. Beat the cream with the sugar until thick.
5. Put the vessel containing the remaining jelly and ice-cream mixture in a larger vessel filled with ice-cubes and go on stirring all the time.
6. When the mixture is slightly thicker, add the beaten cream and sliced strawberries.
7. Stir for 1 minute and pour the mixture over the set jelly. Put to set in the refrigerator.
8. Just before serving, dip the mould in hot water for a few seconds, loosen the sides and unmould on a plate.

  ★ Decorate with strawberries and fresh cream and serve.

APPLE CRUNCH

A warm pudding for the cold season.
Preparation time: 10 minutes · Cooking time: 1 hour · Serves 6 to 8.

8 large dessert apples
10 to 12 pitted black dates
1 teaspoon lemon juice
1 teaspoon cinnamon powder
100 grams (4 oz.) cornflakes
50 grams (2 oz.) margarine or butter
100 grams (4 oz.) sugar

1. Peel the apples and cut into thin slices.
2. Spread the apple slices and dates on a baking dish. Add ½ teacup of water, the lemon juice and cinnamon and half the sugar.
3. Bake in a moderate oven at 350°F for about 30 minutes until the apples are cooked.
4. Crush the cornflakes.
5. Beat the margarine and the balance sugar, add the crushed cornflakes and mix well.
6. Spread this mixture over the apples and bake in a moderate oven at 350°F for about 25 minutes.

  ★ Serve hot with fresh cream or ice-cream.

STRAWBERRY ICE-CREAM PIE

A fitting finale to a grand party.
Preparation time: 10 minutes · Setting time: 30 minutes · Serves 6 to 8.

For the crust
5 to 6 tablespoons coarsely powdered Marie biscuits
4 tablespoons melted margarine *or* butter
1 tablespoon powdered sugar

For the filling
1 family pack (½ litre) strawberry ice-cream
1 packet (11 grams) strong gelatine
200 grams (7 oz.) fresh cream
3 tablespoons powdered sugar
¾ teacup sliced strawberries
cut fruit and cream for decoration

For the crust
1. Mix the ingredients and press well into a 200 or 225 mm. (8" or 9") diameter pie dish.
2. Either chill the crust in the freezer compartment of a refrigerator or bake blind in a hot oven at 400°F for 7 to 8 minutes.

How to proceed
1. Mix the gelatine in 1 teacup of cold water and warm on a slow flame until it dissolves.
2. Soften the strawberry ice-cream.
3. Add the gelatine liquid to the ice-cream. Mix well.
4. Beat the cream with the sugar until thick.
5. Put the ice-cream mixture over hot water and stir until it becomes a smooth sauce. Add the cream and mix well.
6. Add the strawberries, mix well and pour the mixture over the crust. Put to set in the refrigerator.
7. When set, decorate with cream and fruit.

   ★ Cut into slices and serve.

APPLE AND RAISIN PUDDING

A satisfying hot pudding.
Preparation time: 10 minutes · Cooking time: 20 minutes · Serves 6 to 8.

6 large dessert apples
2 tablespoons raisins
6 to 7 tablespoons brown sugar
1 teaspoon cinnamon powder
1 teaspoon lemon juice
rum *or* brandy (optional)
a little butter

1. Soak the raisins in 2 to 3 tablespoons of water or rum for 1 hour.
2. Peel and slice the apples and add to the raisins and liquid.
3. Add the sugar, cinnamon powder and lemon juice and mix. Dot with a little butter.
4. Cover and bake in a hot oven at 450°F for 20 minutes.

   ★ Serve hot.

STRAWBERRY CUSTARD PIE

A lovely dessert for hot days.
Preparation time: 10 minutes · Setting time: 30 minutes · Serves 6 to 8.

For the custard layer
2½ teacups milk
2½ level teaspoons custard powder
5 teaspoons china grass cut into small pieces
9 teaspoons sugar
½ teaspoon vanilla essence
1 200 to 225 mm. (8" to 9") dia. baked pie crust

For the filling
1½ teacups fresh strawberries *or* 1 small can (450 grams) strawberries
2 to 3 tablespoons strawberry jam
a few thin slices fatless sponge cake, *page 168* (optional)
100 grams (4 oz.) fresh cream
2 tablespoons sugar

For the custard layer
1. Mix the custard powder well with ½ teacup of milk.
2. Add the sugar to the rest of the milk, mix and put to boil.
3. When the milk starts boiling, add the custard powder mixture and cook for ½ minute.
4. Mix the china grass with ½ teacup of water in another vessel and cook on a slow flame until the china grass melts. Add this to the custard mixture and mix thoroughly. Strain the mixture and cool until lukewarm.
5. Add the vanilla essence and pour into the pie crust. Allow to set.

For the filling
1. Slice the strawberries.
2. Arrange the cake slices over the custard layer so as to cover it completely.
3. Arrange the strawberry slices over the cake.
4. Melt the jam over a slow flame and brush over the strawberries.
5. Beat the cream and sugar until thick.

How to proceed
1. Pipe or spread the filling over the custard layer.
2. Chill thoroughly in the refrigerator.

★ Cut into slices and serve cold.

Note: You can also use a powdered Marie biscuit crust instead of the baked pie crust.

ORANGE AND LEMON CREAM PICTURE ON PAGE 64

Cool and refreshing.
Preparation time: 10 minutes · Setting time: 30 minutes · Serves 6 to 8.

200 grams (7 oz.) fresh cream
3 tablespoons powdered sugar
1 packet (11 grams) strong gelatine
4 tablespoons orange squash
2 teaspoons lemon juice
1 family pack (½ litre) vanilla ice-cream
½ teaspoon orange essence
a few drops orange colouring
orange segments and cherries for decoration

1. Beat the cream with the sugar until thick.
2. Mix the gelatine in ¾ teacup of cold water and warm on a slow flame until it dissolves.
3. Add the orange squash and lemon juice to the gelatine.
4. Soften the vanilla ice-cream and put in a vessel dipped in hot water.
5. Add the gelatine liquid to the ice-cream and go on stirring until it becomes smooth cream.
6. Remove the mixture from the hot water, add three-quarters of the sweetened cream and mix. Add the orange essence and colouring and mix well.
7. Pour into a soufflé dish or flat dish as desired and put to set in the freezer compartment of a refrigerator.
8. When set, decorate with the remaining sweetened cream and orange segments and cherries.

★ Serve cold.

ORANGE SOUFFLÉ

A tangy soufflé.
Preparation time: 10 minutes · Setting time: 15 minutes · Serves 6.

3 to 4 egg-whites
1 packet (11 grams) strong gelatine
200 grams (7 oz.) fresh cream
6 tablespoons powdered sugar
4 to 5 tablespoons orange squash
2 teaspoons powdered sugar for the cream
grated chocolate for decoration

1. Mix the gelatine in 3 tablespoons of water and warm on a slow flame until it dissolves. Add the orange squash.
2. Beat the cream.
3. Beat the egg-whites stiffly. Gradually beat in the sugar. Add 1 teacup of the beaten cream and the orange squash mixture.
4. Pour into a soufflé dish and chill.
5. Beat the remaining cream with the sugar. Decorate the soufflé with this beaten cream and grated chocolate.

★ Serve chilled.

PEACH AND CREAM PIE

A rich, golden pie.
Preparation time: 10 minutes · Cooking time: 30 minutes · Serves 6 to 8.

115 grams (4 oz.) shortcrust
   pastry dough, *page 165*
1 small can (450 grams)
   peaches
3 tablespoons plain flour
6 tablespoons powdered sugar
½ teaspoon powdered
   cinnamon
¾ teacup fresh cream

1. Roll out the shortcrust pastry dough to fit a 225 mm. (9") diameter pie dish.
2. Put the rolled dough in an ungreased pie dish and prick all over with a fork.
3. Bake blind in a hot oven at 400°F for 7 to 8 minutes.
4. Cool the pastry.
5. Mix the flour and half of the powdered sugar together.
6. Spread half of this mixture evenly on the surface of the pie.
7. Drain the peaches and arrange on top.
8. Beat the cream. Add the remaining sugar mixture to it and mix well.
9. Spread over the peaches and sprinkle the cinnamon on top.
10. Bake in a moderate oven at 350°F for 20 to 25 minutes.

★ Cool, cut into slices and serve.

CHOCOLATE CUPS

Yummy, yummy! Fill with ice-cream for children. For adults, try adding rum to the cream.
Preparation time: 10 minutes · Setting time: 10 minutes · Makes 8 to 10 cups.

For the chocolate cups
5 slabs (100 grams each) plain
   chocolate
2 tablespoons margarine

For the filling
200 grams (7 oz.) fresh cream
3 tablespoons powdered sugar
2 to 3 teacups chopped fruit
   (fresh *or* canned)

For the chocolate cups
1. Melt the chocolate and margarine in a double boiler and mix well.
2. Line small tart moulds with aluminium foil.
3. Apply a little chocolate mixture over each mould. Put to set in the refrigerator.
4. When set, remove the foil and store the chocolate cups in the refrigerator.

How to proceed
1. Beat the cream with the sugar until thick.
2. Fill each chocolate cup with a little cream and fruit.

★ Serve cold.

STRAWBERRY PEACH CRISP

A delightful combination of fruit and jelly.
Preparation time: 15 minutes · Setting time: 30 minutes · Serves 6 to 8.

For the crust
5 to 6 tablespoons coarsely
  powdered Marie biscuits
4 tablespoons melted
  margarine *or* butter
1 tablespoon powdered sugar

For the filling
1 packet (100 grams) strawberry
  jelly
200 grams (7 oz.) fresh cream
3 tablespoons powdered sugar
¾ teacup sliced strawberries
1 small can (450 grams)
  peaches
sweetened cream for decoration

For the crust
1. Mix the ingredients and press well into a
   200 or 225 mm. (8" or 9") diameter pie dish.
2. Either chill the crust in the freezer
   compartment of a refrigerator or bake blind in
   a hot oven at 400°F for 7 to 8 minutes.

For the filling
1. Chop the peaches, leaving 1 or 2 for
   decoration. Keep aside the syrup.
2. Dissolve the jelly in 2 teacups of boiling water.
   Cool and add 1 teacup of the peach syrup.
3. Beat the cream with the sugar until thick.
4. Put the vessel containing the jelly mixture in a
   larger vessel filled with ice-cubes and go on
   stirring all the time.
5. When the mixture gets slightly thicker, add the
   beaten cream, three-quarters of the peaches
   and three-quarters of the strawberries.
   Mix well.

How to proceed
1. When the filling mixture gets thicker again,
   pour over the pie crust. Put to set in the
   refrigerator.
2. When set, decorate with sweetened cream and
   the remaining peaches and strawberries.

   ★ Serve cold.

PINEAPPLE BAVARIAN

Looks grand and tastes good.
Preparation time: 10 minutes · Setting time: 30 minutes · Serves 8.

1 packet (100 grams) pineapple *or* orange jelly
200 grams (7 oz.) fresh cream
3 tablespoons powdered sugar
1 teaspoon lemon juice
1 small can (450 grams) pineapple slices

For decoration
½ packet (of a 100 grams full packet) red coloured jelly

1. Chop the pineapple slices. Keep aside the syrup.
2. Dissolve the pineapple jelly in 2 teacups of boiling water. Cool and add 1 teacup of the pineapple syrup.
3. Beat the cream with the sugar.
4. Put a few pineapple pieces at the bottom of wettened cup cake moulds.
5. Pour a little jelly on top and put to set in the refrigerator.
6. Put the vessel containing the remaining jelly mixture in a larger vessel filled with ice-cubes and go on stirring until the jelly gets thicker.
7. Then add the cream, lemon juice and chopped pineapple and continue stirring.
8. When the mixture gets thicker, pour into the cup moulds. Put to set in the refrigerator.

How to proceed
1. Dissolve the red coloured jelly in 1½ teacups of boiling water.
2. Cool, pour into a flat tray and put to set in a refrigerator.
3. When set, cut into small pieces.
4. Dip the pineapple jelly moulds in hot water for a few seconds, loosen the sides and unmould in a serving plate.

★ Surround with the chopped red jelly and serve.

FACING PAGE
1 LITTLE ALMOND CAKES
2 CHOCOLATE BUTTERFLY CAKES
3 VEGETABLE BUNS
4 CORN AND SPAGHETTI ON TOAST
5 TOSTADAS

STRAWBERRY ICE-CREAM CAKE

A rich cake which can be made in a jiffy.
Preparation time: 10 minutes · No cooking · Serves 8.

1 three-egg fatless sponge cake, *page 168*
5 to 6 tablespoons vanilla ice-cream
200 grams (7 oz.) fresh cream
3 tablespoons powdered sugar
2 teacups strawberries
praline powder, *page 166* (optional)

To be mixed into a syrup
3 teaspoons powdered sugar
½ teacup water
a little rum *or* brandy (optional)

For decoration
strawberries and piped cream

1. Divide the sponge into 2 parts horizontally.
2. Sprinkle the syrup all over the cake and allow to soak.
3. Slice the strawberries, keeping aside a few for decoration.
4. Beat the cream with the sugar until thick.
5. Soften the ice-cream by adding 2 tablespoons of the sweetened cream.
6. Spread firstly the sliced strawberries and next the ice-cream over one part of the cake. Put the other cake part on top.
7. Cover the cake with the sweetened cream. Stick praline powder all over the cake. Decorate with strawberries and a little piped cream on top. Chill.

★ Cut into pieces and serve.

Variation: STRAWBERRY ICE-CREAM CAKE (EGGLESS) Proceed as above using eggless sponge cake, *page 168,* instead of fatless sponge cake.

FACING PAGE
1 CHEESY POTATO GREEN PEA TOAST
2 MEXICAN RAREBIT
3 CASHEWNUT ROCKS
4 CHOCOLATE AND STRAWBERRY SUNDAE
5 FRUIT TARTS

STRAWBERRY AND VANILLA GATEAU

You can make this spectacular gateau in no time at all using any ready-made fatless sponge cake and ice-creams.
Preparation time: 15 minutes · No cooking · Serves 8 to 10.

1 three-egg fatless sponge cake, *page 168*
1 family pack (½ litre) strawberry ice-cream
1 family pack (½ litre) vanilla ice-cream
1 small can (450 grams) pineapple slices

For decoration
100 grams (4 oz.) fresh cream
1½ tablespoons powdered sugar
25 grams (1 oz.) chocolate
1 teacup sliced strawberries
1 teacup mixed fruit pieces
1 tablespoon chopped walnuts

1. Chop the pineapple slices. Keep aside the syrup.
2. Divide the cake horizontally into 3 parts.
3. Place one cake slice in a large bowl and sprinkle syrup over it.
4. Spread the strawberry ice-cream on top and cover with another cake slice.
5. Sprinkle syrup over the second cake slice.
6. Spread the vanilla ice-cream on top.
7. Mix the pineapple and fruit pieces. Sprinkle on top, keeping aside some for decoration. Cover with the last cake slice.
8. Sprinkle syrup on top.
9. Beat the cream with the sugar until thick.
10. Spread the beaten cream over the cake.
11. Melt the chocolate and 2 teaspoons of water in a double boiler.
12. Trickle the melted chocolate over the cream.
13. Sprinkle the nuts on top. Surround with the remaining fruit.
14. Chill the cake thoroughly for at least 3 to 4 hours.

★ Cut into slices and serve cold.

Note: You can change the ice-cream and fruit combinations according to the season, e.g., mango and vanilla ice-creams with mango etc.

Variation: STRAWBERRY AND VANILLA GATEAU (EGGLESS)
Proceed as above using eggless sponge cake, *page 168,* instead of fatless sponge cake.

STRAWBERRY FLAN

Always a hit.
Preparation time: 15 minutes · Cooking time: 30 minutes · Serves 10.

For the flan
1 recipe sponge cake for puddings, *page 166*
3 teacups strawberry *or* vanilla ice-cream
fresh strawberries for decoration

For soaking (the flan)
¾ teacup water
3 teaspoons powdered sugar

For the strawberry sauce
1 teacup strawberry purée
2 level teaspoons cornflour
7 teaspoons sugar
¾ teaspoon lemon juice
a few drops cochineal

For the flan
1. Grease and dust a 175 or 200 mm. (7" or 8") diameter flan tin and pour the cake mixture into it.
2. Bake in a hot oven at 400°F for 12 to 15 minutes.
3. The cake is ready when it leaves the sides of the tin and is springy to touch.
4. Take out from the oven and leave for 1 minute. Invert the tin over a rack and tap sharply to remove.
5. Cool the flan.
6. Mix the sugar and water. Sprinkle a little of this syrup over the flan and allow to soak. Repeat after 10 minutes. Be sure that the flan is moist. Chill.

For the strawberry sauce
1. Mix the cornflour and sugar with 1 teacup of water.
2. Put to cook and go on stirring until the mixture becomes thick and clear.
3. Remove from the fire.
4. Add the strawberry purée, lemon juice and cochineal and mix well.
5. Chill the sauce.

How to serve
When you want to serve, fill the flan with strawberry ice-cream, pour a little strawberry sauce and decorate with fresh strawberries.

★ Cut and serve with extra sauce.

Variation: STRAWBERRY FLAN (EGGLESS) Proceed as above using ingredients for eggless sponge, *page 168,* instead of sponge cake for puddings.

CHOCOLATE PEACH AND PINEAPPLE FLAN

A popular combination.
Preparation time: 15 minutes · Cooking time: 30 minutes · Serves 10 to 12.

1 three-egg fatless chocolate
  sponge cake mixture,
  page 168
1 packet (100 grams) orange
  jelly
1 small can (450 grams)
  pineapple slices
1 small can (450 grams)
  peaches
1 tablespoon orange squash
200 grams (7 oz.) fresh cream
3 tablespoons powdered sugar
cherries for decoration

1. Grease and dust a 225 mm. (9″) diameter flan tin and pour the cake mixture into it.
2. Bake in a hot oven at 400°F for 12 to 15 minutes. The cake is ready when it leaves the sides of the tin and is springy to touch.
3. Remove from the oven and leave for 1 minute. Loosen the sides with a sharp knife. Invert the tin on a rack and tap sharply to remove.
4. Cool the flan.
5. Scoop out a little portion of the cake from the flan.
6. Drain the fruits and keep aside the syrup. Chop the fruits, leaving some for decoration.
7. Soak the flan with a little of the syrup.
8. Dissolve the jelly in 2 teacups of boiling water. Cool and add 1 teacup of the syrup.
9. Put the vessel containing the jelly mixture in a larger vessel filled with ice-cubes and go on stirring all the time.
10. When the mixture gets slightly thicker, add the orange squash and three-quarters of the fruit.
11. Pour over the flan and put to set in the refrigerator.
12. Beat the cream with the sugar, add the remaining fruit and pile on top of the jelly.
13. Decorate with the remaining fruit and cream.

★ Cut into slices and serve cold.

Variation: CHOCOLATE PEACH AND PINEAPPLE FLAN (EGGLESS)
Proceed as above using eggless chocolate sponge cake mixture, *page 167,* instead of the fatless chocolate sponge cake mixture.

CHOCOLATE AND VANILLA GATEAU

PICTURE ON PAGE 36

A classy combination of chocolate cake layers with vanilla ice-cream and raisins and flavoured with brandy.
Preparation time: 30 minutes · Cooking time: 15 minutes · Serves 10.

For the chocolate cake

3 eggs
125 grams (4½ oz.) sugar
85 grams (3 oz.) plain flour
3 teaspoons cocoa
½ teaspoon baking powder

To be mixed into a soaking syrup

1 tablespoon powdered sugar
2 tablespoons brandy
2 tablespoons water

For stuffing and decoration

2 tablespoons raisins
1 family pack (½ litre) vanilla ice-cream
200 grams (7 oz.) fresh cream
3 tablespoons powdered sugar
grated chocolate for decoration

For the chocolate cake

1. Grease a Swiss roll tray with melted margarine or butter. Put grease-proof paper over it and apply the melted fat again.
2. Sieve the flour, cocoa and baking powder together.
3. Beat the eggs and sugar until light and fluffy. Add the flour and mix well.
4. Spread the mixture in the Swiss roll tray and bake in a hot oven at 400°F for 10 to 12 minutes.
5. Cool the cake.

How to proceed

1. Soak the raisins in the soaking syrup for ½ hour. Take out and keep the raisins and the syrup separately.
2. Divide the cake into 3 equal parts horizontally and sprinkle the syrup on all the three parts.
3. Beat the cream with the sugar until thick.
4. Put one slice of the cake in a serving dish. Spread half the ice-cream and half the raisins on top.
5. Put a second slice of cake on top. Similarly spread the remaining ice-cream and raisins.
6. Put the last cake slice on top.
7. Cover the whole cake with the cream and spread plenty of grated chocolate on top.
8. Chill the cake thoroughly for at least 3 to 4 hours.

★ Cut into slices and serve cold.

Variation: CHOCOLATE AND VANILLA GATEAU (EGGLESS) Proceed as above using eggless chocolate sponge cake, *page 167,* instead of the chocolate cake as above.

GATEAU MARGOT

Strawberries, chocolate and cream make a tempting combination.
Preparation time: 20 minutes · Cooking time: 20 minutes · Serves 8.

For the cake

1 three-egg fatless sponge cake mixture, *page 168*
1½ teacups strawberries
150 grams (5 oz.) milk chocolate
300 grams (10½ oz.) fresh cream
4½ tablespoons powdered sugar

To be mixed into a soaking syrup

2 teaspoons sugar
½ teacup water

1. Pour the cake mixture in a well-greased and dusted 175 mm. (7") diameter ring mould tin and bake in a hot oven at 400°F for 15 minutes. The cake is ready when it leaves the sides of the tin and is springy to touch.
2. Cool the cake and divide into 2 parts horizontally.
3. Beat the cream with the sugar until thick.
4. Melt the chocolate in a double boiler and add 2 to 3 tablespoons of the sweetened cream.
5. Sprinkle the syrup over the cake parts and allow to soak.
6. Spread three-fourths of the melted chocolate over one part of the cake.
7. Crush half of the strawberries, add 5 tablespoons of the sweetened cream and spread over the chocolate layer.
8. Place the other cake part on top.
9. Cover with the remaining cream. Decorate with the remaining strawberries and trickle the balance melted chocolate on top.
10. Chill the cake.

★ Cut into slices and serve cold.

Variation: GATEAU MARGOT (EGGLESS) Proceed as above using eggless sponge cake mixture, *page 168,* instead of fatless sponge cake mixture.

GATEAU SUPREME

A terrific-looking cake basket filled with vanilla ice-cream.
Preparation time: 40 minutes · Cooking time: a few minutes · Serves 10.

1 three-egg fatless sponge cake, *page 168,* baked in a 175 mm. (7") dia. ring mould tin
1 small can (450 grams) mixed fruit
200 grams (7 oz.) fresh cream
3 tablespoons powdered sugar
4 teacups vanilla ice-cream
melted praline mixture, *page 166,* and a little oil for the handle
praline powder, *page 166,* for decoration

1. Drain the fruit and keep aside the syrup.
2. Cut the cake into 2 parts horizontally. Soak both parts with fruit syrup.
3. Beat the cream with the sugar until thick.
4. Spread a little cream over one part of the cake and sprinkle some of the fruit over it. Put the other part on top and cover with the remaining cream.
5. Chill thoroughly.
6. To prepare the handle, oil a slab or working surface and 2 knives. Pour the liquid praline mixture on the oiled slab and work it with the knives until it forms a dough. Roll out into a long strip. Thin the strip with a sharp knife. Bend into a U-shaped handle. Cool.

How to serve
Just before serving, sprinkle praline powder on the top and sides of the cake. Fill the centre with the vanilla ice-cream and the remaining fruit. Insert the nougat handle on top.

★ Serve cold after cutting into pieces.

Variation: GATEAU SUPREME (EGGLESS) Proceed as above using eggless sponge cake, *page 168,* instead of fatless sponge cake.

GATEAU CREOLE

A rich gateau with delicious chocolate topping.
Preparation time: 20 minutes · Cooking time: a few minutes · Serves 8.

1 three-egg fatless sponge cake, *page 168*
2 oranges
2 bananas
4 pineapple rings
1 egg-white
100 grams (4 oz.) fresh cream
1½ tablespoons powdered sugar

For the icing
100 grams (4 oz.) plain chocolate
3 tablespoons water
2 teaspoons oil

1. Prepare the fruit. Sprinkle a little sugar over the cut fruit.
2. Beat the egg-white until stiff.
3. Beat the cream with the sugar until thick.
4. Mix the egg-white and the beaten cream.
5. Divide the cake into 2 parts horizontally. Sprinkle the syrup from the pineapple can on the cake parts and allow to soak.
6. Spread half the cream over one part and next spread the fruit over it. Spread the remaining cream over the fruit and put the second cake part on top.
7. Put the chocolate in a double boiler, add the water and oil and cook until the chocolate melts. Spread the melted chocolate on top of the cake.
8. Chill the cake.

★ Serve cold after cutting into pieces.

Variation: GATEAU CREOLE (EGGLESS) Proceed as above using eggless sponge cake, *page 168,* instead of fatless sponge cake.

GATEAU REGENT

Something delicious for preparing when in a hurry.
Preparation time: a few minutes · Cooking time: a few minutes · Serves 6 to 8.

25 to 30 Marie biscuits
2 teaspoons instant coffee
300 grams (10½ oz.) fresh cream
4½ tablespoons powdered sugar
50 grams (2 oz.) chocolate
2 tablespoons chopped walnuts

1. Boil 1 teacup of water, add the coffee and switch off the gas.
2. Beat the cream with the sugar until thick.
3. Melt the chocolate in a double boiler and mix with three-fourths of the beaten cream.
4. Fit a piping bag with a 12 mm. (½") star nozzle and fill with the chocolate cream.
5. Dip the biscuits into the coffee until they lose their crispness.
6. In a serving dish, place 4 to 5 softened biscuits near each other and cover with chocolate cream from the piping bag.
7. Repeat layers of softened biscuits and cream alternately.
8. Decorate with the balance sweetened cream and chopped nuts. Pipe the remaining chocolate cream decoratively around the biscuits and on the sides.

★ Serve cold.

Note: If you like, use ginger biscuits in place of Marie biscuits.

CHERRY CREAM CAKE

A cake with rich cherry pie filling.
Preparation time: 15 minutes · Cooking time: 30 minutes · Serves 10.

1 three-egg fatless sponge cake mixture, *page 168*
1 small can (450 grams) cherries
200 grams (7 oz.) fresh cream
3 tablespoons powdered sugar
a few drops red colouring
1 teaspoon lemon juice
3 teaspoons granulated sugar
2 teaspoons cornflour
2 teaspoons powdered sugar for soaking syrup
grated chocolate for decoration

1. Drain and stone the cherries. Keep aside the syrup.
2. Grease and dust a 200 mm (8") diameter ring mould tin or a 175 mm (7") diameter cake and fill with the cake mixture.
3. Bake in a hot oven at 400°F for 15 to 20 minutes.
4. The cake is ready when it leaves the sides of the tin and is springy to touch.
5. Cool the cake.
6. Divide the cake into 2 parts horizontally.
7. Make a syrup by mixing ½ teacup of cold water very well with the 2 teaspoons of powdered sugar. Soak both parts of the cake thoroughly with this syrup.
8. Mix the cherry syrup, cornflour and granulated sugar. Cook while stirring all the time. When the mixture becomes thick, take off the fire.
9. Keep aside a few cherries for decoration and add the rest to the thick syrup. Cool.
10. Add the lemon juice and colouring.
11. Beat the cream with the sugar until thick.
12. Spread the cherry mixture over one cake half, spread a little cream and put the other half on top.
13. Cover the cake fully with the sweetened cream.
14. Decorate with the balance cherries and the grated chocolate.

★ Cut into slices and serve cold.

Variation: CHERRY CREAM CAKE (EGGLESS) Proceed as above using eggless sponge cake mixture, *page 168,* instead of fatless sponge cake mixture.

FRUIT AND ICE-CREAM CAKE

Curds and ice-cream give a very special taste to this unusual three-tier cake.
Preparation time: 30 minutes · Cooking time: 20 minutes · Serves 10.

½ packet (of a 100 grams full packet) red jelly
1 family pack (½ litre) vanilla ice-cream
1 packet (11 grams) strong gelatine
¾ teacup thick curds
1 small can (450 grams) pineapple slices
1 three-egg fatless sponge cake mixture, *page 168*
2 tablespoons powdered sugar sweetened fresh cream and cherries for decoration

1. Grease and dust a 200 or 225 mm. (8″ or 9″) diameter tin.
2. Pour the cake mixture into it and bake in a hot oven at 400°F for 15 minutes. The cake is ready when it leaves the sides of the tin and is springy to touch.
3. Cool the cake.
4. Divide the cake into 2 parts horizontally. Only one piece is needed for this recipe.
5. Chop the pineapple slices. Use a little of the syrup to soak the cake piece.
6. Take out ¾ teacup of the pineapple syrup, add the gelatine, mix well and heat on a slow flame till the gelatine dissolves.
7. Dissolve the jelly in 1½ teacups of boiling water. Cool. Pour into a tin of the same size used for baking the cake and put to set in the refrigerator.
8. Soften the ice-cream. Add the pineapple pieces, curds, sugar and gelatine liquid and mix well. Put the container in hot water and stir until the mixture becomes a thick, smooth sauce. Pour over the jelly and put to set in the refrigerator.
9. When set, put the cake piece on top.

How to serve
To serve, dip the tin in hot water for a few seconds, loosen the sides and unmould on a plate. Pipe the sweetened cream all round. Decorate with cherries.

★ Cut into slices and serve cold.

Variation: FRUIT AND ICE-CREAM CAKE (EGGLESS) Proceed as above using eggless sponge cake mixture, *page 168,* instead of fatless sponge cake mixture.

NOUGAT CAKE <small>PICTURE ON PAGE 81</small>

This cake makes a superb dessert.
Preparation time: 20 minutes · Cooking time: 20 minutes · Serves 8.

1 three-egg fatless sponge cake mixture, *page 168*
300 grams (10½ oz.) fresh cream
4½ tablespoons powdered sugar
1 small can (450 grams) pineapple slices
1 small slab (50 grams) chocolate
praline powder, *page 166*
a knob butter
cherries and pineapple slices for decoration

1. Grease and dust a 175 or 200 mm. (7" or 8") diameter ring mould tin and pour the cake mixture into it.
2. Bake in a hot oven at 400°F for 15 to 20 minutes. The cake is ready when it leaves the sides of the tin and is springy to touch.
3. Take out from the oven and leave for 1 minute. Loosen the sides with a knife and invert over a rack, tapping sharply to remove.
4. Cool the cake.
5. Chop the pineapple slices, keeping aside 1 slice for decoration. Keep aside the syrup.
6. Chop half of the chocolate into small pieces.
7. Divide the cake into 2 parts horizontally.
8. Sprinkle a little pineapple syrup over both the cake parts and allow to soak. Repeat after 10 minutes. Be sure that the cake is moist.
9. Beat the cream with the powdered sugar until thick.
10. Mix 4 tablespoons of the beaten cream with the chopped chocolate and chopped pineapple pieces.
11. Spread this mixture over one cake part and put the other cake part on top.
12. Cover the cake on all sides with the cream.
13. Sprinkle the praline powder on top.
14. Melt the remaining chocolate in a double boiler. Add a little water and a knob of butter. Trickle this chocolate over the cake.
15. Pipe the remaining cream on top.
16. Decorate with cherries and pineapple slices. Chill thoroughly.

★ Cut into slices and serve cold.

Variation: NOUGAT CAKE (EGGLESS) Proceed as above using eggless sponge cake mixture, *page 168,* instead of fatless sponge cake mixture.

X. Biscuits and Pastries

COCONUT BISCUITS

Tea-time biscuits.
Preparation time: 15 minutes · Cooking time: 20 minutes · Makes 15 to 20 biscuits.

115 grams (4 oz.) soft margarine *or* butter
55 grams (2 oz.) powdered sugar
170 grams (6 oz.) plain flour
25 grams (1 oz.) desiccated coconut
1 teaspoon vanilla essence
jam and vanilla butter icing, *page 167,* for decoration

1. Cream the margarine and sugar very well until light and creamy.
2. Add the vanilla essence and beat again.
3. Add the flour and desiccated coconut and mix well.
4. Make small balls from the dough.
5. Arrange on a greased baking tin. Press the thumb in the centre of each ball and make a dent.
6. Bake in a moderate oven at 350°F for 20 minutes.
7. Cool the biscuits.

   ★ Put jam in the centre of each biscuit, pipe the icing on the border and serve.

SWEET COCONUT TOAST

It is difficult to believe that this unusual toast is made from bread.
Preparation time: a few minutes · Cooking time: 25 minutes · Makes 12 pieces.

a few bread slices
1 teacup condensed milk
1 teacup desiccated coconut

1. Toast the bread slices.
2. Cut into thin fingers.
3. Dip the toast fingers in condensed milk and then roll into the coconut.
4. Arrange the fingers on a very well-greased baking tray.
5. Bake in a hot oven at 300°F for 15 to 20 minutes.

   ★ Serve hot or cold.

113

COCONUT ROCKS

So easy to make!

Preparation time: a few minutes · Cooking time: 20 minutes · Makes 8 to 10 rocks.

1 teacup condensed milk
1 teacup desiccated coconut
glacé cherries for decoration

1. Mix the milk and coconut.
2. Put a little mixture in a paper cup and put a small piece of cherry on top. Repeat for the rest of the mixture.
3. Bake in a hot oven at 400°F for 15 to 20 minutes.
4. Cool.

Variation: COCONUT COOKIES

1 teacup condensed milk
1½ to 2 teacups desiccated coconut
glacé cherries for decoration

1. Mix the milk and coconut. This mixture should be a little stiff.
2. Make small balls of the mixture and arrange on a greased baking tray. Make a small dent on each ball and put a piece of cherry in it.
3. Bake in a moderate oven at 350°F for 25 minutes.
4. Cool.

CHOCOLATE PASTRIES

Chocolate biscuit cups filled with cream, sugar and fruit.

Preparation time: 20 minutes · Cooking time: 30 minutes · Makes 10 to 12 pieces.

75 grams (2¾ oz.) plain flour
2 teaspoons cocoa
75 grams (2¾ oz.) butter
30 grams (1 oz.) icing sugar
1 teaspoon vanilla essence
200 grams (7 oz.) fresh cream
3 tablespoons powdered sugar
2 teacups mixed fruit pieces
fresh grapes, cherries, strawberries for decoration

1. Sieve the flour and cocoa together.
2. Beat the butter and icing sugar very well.
3. Add the vanilla essence and beat again.
4. Add the flour and mix well.
5. Fit a 12 mm. (½") star nozzle to a piping bag filled with the mixture and pipe rounds in individual paper cups.
6. Bake in a moderate oven at 350°F for 25 to 30 minutes.
7. Cool the pastries.
8. Beat the cream and powdered sugar.
9. Fill the pastries with fruit pieces and pipe the sweetened cream on top. Decorate some pastries with grapes, others with cherries and the rest with strawberries.

CHELSEA BUNS

A traditional tea-time fare which requires a skilled hand to make.
Preparation time: 15 minutes · Cooking time: 25 minutes · Makes 10 to 12 buns.

15 grams (½ oz.) fresh yeast *or*
  2 level teaspoons dry yeast
75 grams (3 oz.) powdered
  sugar
150 ml. (5 fl. oz.) milk
350 grams (12 oz.) plain flour
100 grams (4 oz.) margarine
a pinch salt
75 grams (3 oz.) mixed dried
  fruit (chopped)
25 grams (1 oz.) orange peel
  (chopped)

For the glaze
25 grams (1 oz.) powdered
  sugar
1 tablespoon water

1. Cream the yeast with 1 teaspoon of sugar.
2. Warm the milk and add to the mixture.
3. Sprinkle a little flour on top. Cover and keep until bubbles come on top.
4. Sieve the flour with a pinch of salt. Rub in 50 grams of margarine. Add 25 grams of sugar.
5. Add the yeast liquid and some more warm water. Make a soft dough.
6. Knead for 7 minutes. Keep under a wet cloth until double in size (this takes at least 30 minutes).
7. Knead the dough again and divide into 2 parts. Roll out each part into an oblong shape.
8. Warm the remaining margarine slightly and apply on the above parts.
9. Sprinkle the chopped fruits and peel. Sprinkle the balance sugar.
10. Roll up tightly like a Swiss roll. Cut into slices and arrange on a greased baking tray. Store in a closed cupboard until double in size.
11. Bake in a hot oven at 450°F for 15 to 20 minutes.
12. Just before removing from the oven, mix the sugar and water. Apply this glaze on the hot buns and put back in the oven for a few minutes.

★ Serve warm or cold.

FRUIT TARTS PICTURE ON PAGE 100

Try these tarts with different combinations of fruit and jelly. Excellent for tea parties.
Preparation time: 45 minutes · Cooking time: 15 minutes · Makes 12 tarts.

For the tart cases
225 grams (8 oz.) shortcrust
  pastry dough, *page 165*

For the filling
1 small can (450 grams)
  pineapple slices
½ packet (of a 100 grams full
  packet) raspberry *or*
  strawberry jelly
1 teacup chopped fresh fruit

For decoration
200 grams (7 oz.) fresh cream
3 tablespoons powdered sugar

For the tart cases
1. Roll out the pastry dough. Cut with a fluted
   cutter. Press into tart forms. Prick all over with
   a fork.
2. Bake blind in a hot oven at 400°F for
   10 to 15 minutes. Cool.

For the filling
1. Chop the pineapple slices. Keep aside the
   syrup.
2. Dissolve the jelly in 1 teacup of boiling water.
   Cool and add the pineapple syrup.
3. Put the vessel containing the jelly mixture in a
   larger vessel filled with ice-cubes and go on
   stirring all the time.
4. When the mixture becomes thicker, add
   three-quarters of fruit and mix well.

How to proceed
1. Pour the jelly into the tart cases. Put to set in a
   refrigerator.
2. Beat the cream with the sugar until thick.
3. When set, pipe the cream on top and decorate
   with the balance fruit.

VANILLA FORK BISCUITS

They really taste superb.
Preparation time: 15 minutes · Cooking time: 25 minutes · Makes about 25 biscuits.

150 grams (5¼ oz.) plain flour
100 grams (3½ oz.) unsalted butter
60 grams (2 oz.) powdered sugar
½ teaspoon vanilla essence

1. Sieve the flour.
2. Cream the butter and sugar very well until light and creamy.
3. Add the vanilla essence and mix well.
4. Add the flour and make a dough.
5. Roll into small round balls and arrange on a greased baking tray.
6. Press with a wet fork.
7. Bake in a moderate oven at 350°F for 20 to 25 minutes.

Variation 1: COCONUT FORK BISCUITS Add 25 grams (1 oz.) of desiccated coconut to the mixture at step 3.
Variation 2: CHOCOLATE FORK BISCUITS Add 1½ teaspoons of cocoa to the mixture at step 3.

EGGLESS MACAROONS

You won't believe that these delicious macaroons are made without eggs.
Preparation time: 20 minutes · Cooking time: 30 minutes · Makes about 25 macaroons.

100 grams (3½ oz.) plain flour
50 grams (2 oz.) desiccated coconut
25 grams (1 oz.) ghee
25 grams (1 oz.) fine semolina
85 grams (3 oz.) granulated sugar
½ level teaspoon baking ammonia
½ teaspoon cardamom powder
1 teaspoon liquid ghee

1. Heat the liquid ghee in a tava or skillet, add the cardamom powder and coconut and roast for 1 minute.
2. Add the ammonia to 100 ml. (3 fl. oz.) water and mix well.
3. Beat the ghee and sugar. Add 2 teaspoons of the ammonia solution and beat very well again.
4. Add the plain flour, semolina, coconut mixture and remaining ammonia solution and mix well.
5. Oil a baking tray and put the mixture on it in the form of small lumps. Bake in a preheated moderate oven at 350°F for 25 to 30 minutes.
6. Cool the macaroons.

117

CASHEWNUT ROCKS PICTURE ON PAGE 100

Rich rocks which melt in your mouth.
Preparation time: 15 minutes · Cooking time: 30 minutes · Makes 15 to 20 rocks.

100 grams (3½ oz.) plain flour
2 to 3 tablespoons chopped
cashewnuts
100 grams (3½ oz.) butter *or*
margarine
50 grams (1¾ oz.) powdered
sugar
2 to 3 drops almond essence *or*
1 teaspoon vanilla essence
3 to 4 chopped glacé cherries

1. Sieve the flour.
2. Spread the cashewnut pieces on a tray and chop finely. Bake in a hot oven at 400°F for 10 minutes.
3. Beat the butter and sugar very well until light and creamy.
4. Add the essence and beat again.
5. Add the flour and mix well.
6. Form into small balls and roll into the cashewnuts.
7. Bake in a moderate oven at 350°F for 25 to 30 minutes.
8. Cool the biscuits and place glacé cherry pieces on top.

Variation: COCONUT AND WALNUT ROCKS Instead of chopped cashewnuts, use 2 to 3 tablespoons of desiccated coconut and 1 tablespoon of chopped walnuts. Omit step 2 and at step 6, roll into the desiccated coconut and chopped walnuts.

CHOCOLATE COOKIES

Children's favourite.
Preparation time: 15 minutes · Cooking time: 20 minutes · Makes about 30 cookies.

85 grams (3 oz.) plain flour
85 grams (3 oz.) butter *or*
margarine
55 grams (2 oz.) icing sugar
25 grams (1 oz.) cornflour
1½ teaspoons cocoa
1 teaspoon vanilla essence
2 tablespoons milk
a pinch salt

1. Sieve the plain flour, cornflour, cocoa and salt together.
2. Cream the butter and sugar very well until light and creamy.
3. Add the vanilla essence and mix well.
4. Add the flour mixture and mix well.
5. Add the milk and mix well.
6. Fit a 12 mm. (½") star nozzle to a piping bag filled with the mixture and pipe the mixture in circles on a greased baking tin.
7. Bake in a moderate oven at 350°F for 20 minutes.

Variation 1: VANILLA COOKIES Proceed as above omitting cocoa.
Variation 2: COFFEE COOKIES Proceed as above using 1 teaspoon of instant coffee instead of the cocoa.

SHORTBREAD FLAPJACKS

A lovely tea-time pastry.
Preparation time: 20 minutes · Cooking time: 30 minutes · Makes 10 to 12 pieces.

For the shortbread
115 grams (4 oz.) plain flour
55 grams (2 oz.) butter
55 grams (2 oz.) sugar
very little milk

For the topping
40 grams (1½ oz.) soft
   margarine
1 tablespoon golden syrup
55 grams (2 oz.) cornflakes
25 grams (1 oz.) sugar
55 grams (2 oz.) rolled oats

For the shortbread
1. Cream the butter and sugar very well till light and creamy.
2. Add the flour and a few drops of milk.
3. Make a dough.
4. Roll out the dough to 6 mm. (¼") thickness and make an oblong shape.

For the topping
1. Melt the margarine and golden syrup in a vessel.
2. Stir in the cornflakes, sugar and the rolled oats. Mix well.

How to proceed
1. Place the shortbread dough on an ungreased baking tin and press the topping mixture firmly on top.
2. Bake in the centre of a moderate oven at 375°F for 25 minutes.
3. Mark into fingers while hot, but leave on the tin until quite cool.

CHOCOLATE BUTTERFLY CAKES PICTURE ON PAGE 99

Highly attractive.
Preparation time: 20 minutes · Cooking time : 20 minutes · Makes 8 to 10 cakes.

2 large eggs
115 grams (4 oz.) soft margarine
  or butter
115 grams (4 oz.) powdered
  sugar
170 grams (6 oz.) plain flour
1 level teaspoon baking powder
1 teaspoon cocoa
1 teaspoon vanilla essence or
  ½ teaspoon lemon essence
vanilla butter icing, *page 167*
icing sugar

1. Sieve the flour.
2. Beat the margarine and sugar very well until light and fluffy.
3. Beat the eggs until fluffy.
4. Add the beaten eggs, a little at a time, to the margarine and go on beating each time.
5. Add the flour, baking powder, cocoa and essence. Add a little water to get a dropping consistency.
6. Fill the paper cups upto three-quarter height with the mixture and bake in a hot oven at 400°F for 20 minutes.
7. Cool the cakes.
8. Cut a piece from the centre of each cake. Fill the cavities with butter icing.
9. Divide the removed pieces into half, dust with icing sugar and press the cut pieces into the icing at an angle to form the wings of a butterfly. Pipe a little more icing between the wings.

LITTLE ALMOND CAKES PICTURE ON PAGE 99

A wonderful combination of nuts, cream and jam.
Preparation time: 15 minutes · Cooking time: 20 minutes · Makes 20 to 25 cakes.

85 grams (3 oz.) soft margarine
  or butter
85 grams (3 oz.) powdered
  sugar
⅙ teaspoon almond essence
  (approx.)
2 teaspoons plain flour
115 grams (4 oz.) powdered
  almonds or cashewnuts
jam and sweetened cream for
  decoration

1. Cream the margarine and sugar very well until light and creamy.
2. Add the almond essence and mix well.
3. Add the plain flour and nuts and mix well.
4. Put the mixture in paper cups, 1 teaspoon to a cup.
5. Arrange the paper cups on a baking tin and bake in a moderate oven at 350°F for about 20 minutes.
6. Fill the centres which are formed in the cakes with cream and put a dot of jam (or cherry) on top.

MEXICAN RAREBIT PICTURE ON PAGE 100

Spicy and good-looking.
Preparation time: 15 minutes · Cooking time: 25 minutes · Makes 12 to 15 pieces.

For the toast cases
10 to 15 slices bread
a little butter

For the filling
1 packet frozen corn *or*
   3 teacups cooked corn
3 large tomatoes
1 chopped onion
1 chopped capsicum
3 finely chopped green chillies
3 tablespoons oil
salt to taste

For baking
¾ teacup tomato ketchup
3 tablespoons grated cheese

For the toast cases
1. Remove the crust from the bread slices.
2. Roll out a little and press into the cavities of a muffin tray which is greased with butter.
3. Brush with melted butter and bake in a hot oven at 450°F for 10 minutes or until crisp.

For the filling
1. Put the tomatoes in hot water. After 10 minutes, take off the skin and chop.
2. Heat the oil and fry the onions till light pink in colour.
3. Add the capsicum, green chillies and chopped tomatoes and fry for at least 3 to 4 minutes.
4. Add the corn and salt.

How to proceed
Fill a little mixture in each toast case, spread a little tomato ketchup and sprinkle cheese on top. Bake in a hot oven at 400°F for 5 to 10 minutes or until the cheese melts.

★ Serve hot.

APPLE BURGER

A very different and light burger.
Preparation time: 20 minutes · Cooking time: 20 minutes · Makes 10 to 12 burgers.

For the burger
1 teacup finely chopped french beans
1 teacup finely chopped carrot
1 teacup finely chopped cabbage
½ teacup green peas
3 boiled and mashed potatoes
1 chopped onion
2 tablespoons chopped coriander
4 to 5 chopped green chillies
¼ teaspoon turmeric powder
½ teaspoon garam masala
bread crumbs
2 tablespoons oil
salt to taste
oil for frying

For the base and topping
apple slices
tomato slices
onion rings
½ teacup tomato ketchup mixed with 2 teaspoons chilli sauce
1 teaspoon mustard powder mixed with a little water

For the burger
1. Heat the oil and fry the onion for 1 minute.
2. Add the french beans, carrot, cabbage, green pea, turmeric powder, garam masala and salt. Cover and cook until the vegetables are soft.
3. Add the potatoes, coriander and green chillies and mix.
4. Cool the mixture.
5. Shape into rounds and flatten. Roll into bread crumbs and cook on a tava with a little oil.

How to serve
On each apple slice, put one burger. Apply a little tomato-chilli sauce and mustard to the burger and top with a tomato slice and onion ring.

★ Serve hot.

VEGETABLE HOT DOGS

For the young people in a hurry.
Preparation time: 10 minutes · Cooking time : 15 minutes · Makes 12 hot dogs.

12 hot dog rolls
1 chopped onion
2 chopped tomatoes
1 large chopped capsicum
1 teacup cooked rice
1 teacup grated cheese
½ teaspoon chilli powder
1 tablespoon butter
salt to taste
butter for applying to the rolls

1. Slit open the rolls lengthwise. Scoop out the centres on one side.
2. Heat the butter and fry the onion for 1 minute. Add the tomatoes and capsicum and cook for 1 minute.
3. Mix the rice, cheese, cooked vegetables, chilli powder and salt.
4. Fill the scooped portions of the rolls with this stuffing.
5. Apply butter on the outside of the rolls. Bake in a hot oven at 400°F for 10 minutes.

  ★ Serve hot.

SPINACH ROLLS

A novel snack, easy to prepare.
Preparation time: 10 minutes · Cooking time: 10 minutes · Makes 20 to 30 small rolls.

25 to 30 spinach leaves
4 boiled and mashed potatoes
1½ teaspoons amchur powder
1 chopped onion
3 chopped green chillies
1 tablespoon ghee
salt to taste
oil for deep frying
tomato ketchup for serving

For the batter
½ teacup gram flour
½ teacup rice flour *or* plain flour
½ teaspoon chilli powder
½ teaspoon salt
1 teacup water

1. Heat the ghee and fry the onion for 1 minute. Add the green chillies and fry again for a few seconds.
2. Add the potatoes, amchur powder and salt. Cool and shape into rolls.
3. Put a small roll of the potato filling in the centre of a spinach leaf and wrap the leaf round the potato roll. Repeat for the remaining filling and spinach leaves.
4. Mix the ingredients for the batter, dip the rolls in this batter and deep fry in oil.

  ★ Serve hot with tomato ketchup.

Note: If the spinach leaves are too large, cut into small rectangular pieces.

Variation: You can also use 1½ teacups of crumbled paneer in place of the potatoes.

CHEESY POTATO GREEN PEA TOAST

PICTURE ON PAGE 100

Colourful, attractive and tasty too.
Preparation time: 15 minutes · Cooking time: 20 minutes · Makes 12 to 14 toasts.

12 to 14 round pieces toast
4 boiled and mashed potatoes
1 teacup milk
1 teaspoon butter
1 teacup boiled green peas
2 to 3 chopped green chillies
¼ teaspoon pepper powder
salt to taste
oil for frying

For the cheese covering
4 tablespoons cornflour
2 tablespoons grated cooking
   cheese
2 pinches baking powder
½ teacup milk
1 teaspoon mustard powder
¼ teaspoon pepper powder
salt to taste

For serving
tomato ketchup

1. Mix the potatoes, milk, butter, green peas, green chillies, pepper and salt.
2. Mix all the ingredients for the cheese covering.
3. On each piece of toast, spread the potato mixture evenly. Make a small hole in the centre.
4. Apply the cheese covering all over the potato mixture and seal the edges between the potato mixture and toast.
5. Deep fry upside down in hot oil.

   ★ Fill the centre with tomato ketchup and serve.

VEGETABLE BUNS PICTURE ON PAGE 99

Quick, attractive and tasty.
Preparation time: 20 minutes · Cooking time: 30 minutes · Makes 12 buns.

For the buns
6 bread buns
a little butter *or* margarine

For the stuffing
2 teacups mixed boiled
  vegetables (french beans,
  carrots, green peas)
1 boiled and mashed potato
1 chopped tomato
2 tablespoons chopped
  coriander
½ teaspoon chilli powder
1 chopped onion
2 tablespoons oil
tomato ketchup
salt to taste

**To be ground into a paste
  (for the stuffing)**
1 onion
4 green chillies
25 mm. (1") piece ginger

For baking
tomato ketchup
2 tablespoons grated cheese

For the buns
1. Divide each bun horizontally into 2 halves.
2. Scoop out the centre of each half and apply a little melted butter on the inside.
3. Bake in a hot oven at 450°F for 10 to 15 minutes or until crisp.

For the stuffing
1. Heat the oil and fry the onion for 1 minute.
2. Add the paste and fry again for 1 minute.
3. Add the tomato, coriander, chilli powder, tomato ketchup and salt and fry for 1 minute.
4. Add the vegetables and potato and mix well.

How to proceed
Fill the bun centres with the stuffing. Spread a little tomato ketchup and grated cheese on the buns and bake in a hot oven at 450°F for 10 minutes.

★ Serve hot.

CHAAT BASKET

A three-in-one taste — khatta, mitha, tikha — for the spice lovers.
Preparation time: 40 to 50 minutes · Cooking time: 40 minutes · Serves 12.

For the baskets
400 grams (14 oz.) plain flour
5 tablespoons ghee
½ teaspoon salt
oil for frying

For the green chutney
1½ teacups chopped coriander
6 green chillies
25 mm. (1") piece ginger
1 teaspoon cumin seeds
salt to taste

For the sweet chutney
1 teacup tamarind
2 teacups dates
1 teaspoon chilli powder
1 teaspoon roasted cumin
   powder
2 pinches black salt
salt to taste

For filling No. 1
1 teacup sprouted math
1 tablespoon oil
2 bay leaves
1 teaspoon cumin seeds
½ teaspoon chilli powder
salt to taste

For filling No. 2
4 boiled and mashed potatoes
2 chopped green chillies
½ teaspoon red chilli powder
½ teaspoon cumin powder
1 tablespoon chopped
   coriander
salt to taste

For the baskets
1. Mix all the ingredients and make a fairly stiff
   dough by adding water. Knead well.
2. Roll out small puris and press over a tart
   mould. Deep fry in hot oil.

For the green chutney
   Make a paste of all the ingredients. Add 1
   teacup of water and mix well.

For the sweet chutney
1. Soak the dates in 1 teacup of water. Soak the
   tamarind separately.
2. When soaked, remove the seeds. Blend the
   rest in a liquidiser. Strain.
3. Add the roasted cumin powder, chilli powder,
   black salt and salt.

For filling No. 1
1. Heat the oil.
2. Add the bay leaves and cumin seeds and fry
   for ½ minute.
3. Add the math, chilli powder and salt.

For filling No. 2
Mix all the ingredients.

For filling No. 3
1. Put the bundi in lukewarm water for 1 minute.
2. Drain and divide it into 3 parts.
3. Churn the curds.
4. Put 1 part each in curds, green chutney and in
   sweet chutney.

How to serve
   In each basket, put a little of each of the three
   fillings — firstly a little math, then a little
   potato mixture and lastly 3 coloured bundis.

★ Sprinkle sev, coriander and chilli powder and
serve.

For filling No. 3
300 grams (11 oz.) besan bundi
1 teacup fresh curds

For the garnish
sev, chopped coriander, chilli
    powder

Note: Instead of baskets, you can use the ready-made canapé packets available in the market.

QUICK PIZZA

A quick and simple version of the traditional dish.
Preparation time: 15 minutes · Cooking time: 15 minutes · Makes 4 to 5 small pizzas.

For the dough
200 grams (7 oz.) plain flour
2 level teaspoons baking
    powder
2 teaspoons oil
½ teaspoon salt

For the topping
4 large tomatoes
2 sliced onions
4 cloves crushed garlic
2 pinches ajwain *or* ½ teaspoon
    oregano
1 teaspoon sugar
½ teaspoon chilli powder
1 tablespoon oil
salt to taste

For spreading and cooking
100 grams (4 oz.) grated
    cooking cheese
a few capsicum rings
a little butter
salt and chilli powder to taste
oil for frying

1. Mix together all the ingredients of the dough and make a dough by adding water.
2. Put the tomatoes into hot water for about 10 minutes. Remove the skins and slice them.
3. Heat the oil and fry the onions for 2 minutes.
4. Add the garlic and fry again for a few seconds.
5. Add the tomato slices, ajwain, sugar, chilli powder and salt and cook for a few minutes.

How to proceed
1. Divide the dough into 4 to 5 equal parts. Roll out about 6 mm. (¼") chapatis and prick slightly.
2. Heat 1 to 2 tablespoons of oil in a frying pan. Put 1 chapati in the pan and when cooked on one side, turn on the other side. Spread a little filling and sprinkle plenty of cheese on top. Put a few capsicum rings, dot with butter, sprinkle salt and chilli powder and cook for 2 minutes. Then put below the grill (or in an oven) until the cheese melts.
3. Repeat with the remaining chapatis.

★ Serve hot.

TOSTADAS PICTURE ON PAGE 99

A vegetarian version of a Mexican snack.
Preparation time: 40 minutes · Cooking time: 40 minutes · Makes about 30 pieces.

For the tostadas
2 teacups plain flour
2 teacups maize flour
4 teaspoons oil
¾ teaspoon salt
oil for deep frying

For the stuffing
1 small can (450 grams) baked
  beans
1 boiled potato
1 chopped onion
1 teacup mixed boiled
  vegetables (french beans,
  carrots, green peas)
1 teaspoon chilli powder
3 tablespoons oil
salt to taste

For serving
fresh green salad with french
  dressing
grated cabbage and carrots
  with salad cream, *page 164*
grated cheese
chillies in vinegar

For the tostadas
1. Mix both the flours, add the salt and oil and
   enough water to make a dough.
2. Roll into small thick puris with the help of a
   little plain flour. Prick with a fork and deep fry
   in oil until crisp.

For the stuffing
1. Cut the potatoes into small pieces.
2. Heat the oil and fry the onion for 1 minute.
3. Add the remaining ingredients and cook for a
   little time.

How to serve
On each tostada, spread a little stuffing,
sprinkle either of the salads with dressing.

★ Sprinkle grated cheese and chillies in vinegar
  and serve.

CORN AND SPAGHETTI ON TOAST PICTURE ON PAGE 99

This combination of East and West makes a tasty and filling snack.
Preparation time: 30 minutes · Cooking time: 15 minutes · Makes about 15 pieces.

1 medium loaf sliced bread
2 teacups cooked corn
2 teacups cooked spaghetti
1 chopped onion
2 tablespoons milk
2 tablespoons fresh cream
2 teacups white sauce, *page 164*
4 tablespoons grated cooking
  cheese
tomato slices
a little butter
2 tablespoons ghee
salt and pepper to taste

To be ground into a paste
4 green chillies
4 cloves garlic
¾ teacup chopped coriander
12 mm. (½") piece ginger

1. Apply butter to the bread slices and toast them.
2. Heat the ghee and fry the onion for ½ minute.
3. Add the paste and fry again for 2 to 3 minutes.
4. Add the corn, milk, cream and salt.
5. Mix the spaghetti and white sauce. Add salt and pepper and half the cheese.
6. On each toast, spread a layer of the corn mixture first and then a layer of the spaghetti mixture. Cover with tomato slices and sprinkle the balance cheese on top.
7. Bake in a hot oven at 450°F for 10 minutes.

  ★ Serve hot.

PANEER TOAST

A protein-packed breakfast snack.
Preparation time: a few minutes · Cooking time: a few minutes · Makes 6 pieces.

6 brown bread slices
100 grams (4 oz.) paneer
1 chopped green chilli
2 pinches salt
a little butter

1. Crumble the paneer and add the chilli and salt.
2. Sandwich the bread slices with the paneer mixture without using any butter.
3. Apply a little butter on either side of the sandwiches.
4. Toast the sandwiches in a sandwich toaster or by cooking on a griddle until crisp and brown on either side.

  ★ Cut into two and serve hot.

STUFFED MOONG DAL CHILAS

A novel and tastier version of the traditional chila.
Preparation time: 20 minutes · Cooking time: 30 minutes · Makes 15 large chilas.

For the stuffing
2 boiled potatoes, cut into cubes
1 teacup boiled green peas
1 teaspoon cumin seeds
2 chopped green chillies
1 to 2 teaspoons amchur
    powder
1 tablespoon ghee
salt to taste

For the chilas
2 teacups moong dal
4 green chillies
a pinch asafoetida
salt to taste
ghee for cooking
green chutney and sweet
    chutney to serve

For the stuffing
1. Heat the ghee and fry the cumin seeds for
   ½ minute.
2. Add the remaining ingredients and cook for a
   few minutes. Mash.

For the chila mixture
1. Soak the moong dal for at least 3 hours.
2. Blend in a liquidiser with the green chillies and
   1 teacup of water.
3. Add the asafoetida and salt.

How to proceed
1. Spread a little moong dal mixture on a frying
   pan (preferably non-stick). Smear a little ghee
   around the mixture.
2. Spread a little stuffing over the uncooked side
   and cook.
3. When the side in contact with the pan is
   brown, turn over and cook the other side till
   brown.
4. Repeat for the rest of the mixture.

   ★ Serve hot with green and sweet chutneys.

MOONG DAL PANKI

A snack for Sunday mornings.
Preparation time: 20 minutes · Cooking time: 20 to 30 minutes · Makes 15 to 20 pankis.

200 grams (7 oz.) moong dal with skin
1 boiled and chopped potato
¾ teacup boiled green peas
6 to 7 green chillies
2 pinches asafoetida
½ teaspoon sugar
½ teaspoon soda bi-carb
1 tablespoon oil
2 tablespoons chopped coriander
sweet chutney and green chutney to serve

1. Soak the moong dal for 3 to 4 hours. Rinse and drain.
2. Add the chillies and ¾ teacup of water and blend in a liquidiser.
3. Add the potato, green peas, asafoetida, sugar, soda bi-carb, oil and coriander and mix well.
4. Cut banana leaves into squares of about 150 or 175 mm. (6" or 7") and grease with a little oil on one side. Spread about 1 tablespoon of the mixture over the greased side of a leaf square and cover with the greased side of another leaf.
5. Cook on a tava on each side for 1 to 2 minutes. Repeat with the rest of the mixture.

★ Serve hot (without removing the leaves) in individual plates with sweet and green chutneys. Just before eating, remove the pankis steaming from the leaves and apply the chutneys.

Note: You can also use corn leaves if banana leaves are not available.

PASTA TOAST

Serve as a children's snack or as a light evening snack.
Preparation time: 10 minutes · Cooking time: 15 minutes · Makes 20 toasts.

20 bread slices (buttered on one side)
2 teacups cooked letter macaroni
1 chopped onion
½ teacup tomato ketchup
4 to 5 chopped green chillies
1 to 2 teaspoons chilli sauce (optional)
3 to 4 tablespoons grated cheese
2 tablespoons butter *or* ghee
salt to taste

1. Heat the butter and fry the onion for 1 minute. Add the macaroni, tomato ketchup, green chillies, chilli sauce, cheese and salt and mix well.
2. Sandwich the macaroni stuffing between bread slices in such a way that the buttered sides are on the outside.
3. Cook the sandwiches on a tava (or skillet) until brown on either side.

★ Cut into two and serve hot.

CREAMED CABBAGE SNACK

Even those who do not care for cabbage will enjoy this snack.
Preparation time: 15 minutes · Cooking time: 20 minutes · Makes 20 pieces.

20 cream cracker biscuits *or*
    20 pieces toast
20 cabbage leaves
1½ teacups finely chopped
    mixed boiled vegetables
    (french beans, carrots,
    cauliflower)
2 boiled and sliced potatoes
1½ teacups white sauce,
    page 164
1 chopped green chilli
2 tablespoons butter
4 tablespoons grated cheese
salt and pepper to taste
tabasco sauce to serve

1. Put plenty of water to boil and add 2 teaspoons of salt.
2. When the water starts boiling, switch off the gas and add the cabbage leaves.
3. After a few minutes, drain out the water. Cut out rounds and chop the rest of the cabbage.
4. Heat the butter and fry the cabbage leaves for 1 minute.
5. Add the boiled vegetables, chopped cabbage, the green chilli, 1 teacup of white sauce, salt, pepper and half of the cheese. Mix well.
6. On each biscuit (or toast), first put a leaf of cabbage. Pile the vegetables on top. Put a slice of potato on top. Cover with white sauce. Sprinkle the remaining cheese.
7. Bake in a hot oven at 400°F for 10 minutes.

★ Serve hot with tabasco sauce.

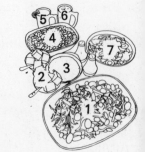

FACING PAGE
1 FRUIT AND VEGETABLE SALAD
2 WATER-MELON ICE
3 DIETERS' THOUSAND ISLAND DRESSING
4 BAKED PANEER WITH VEGETABLES
5 VITAMIN CUP
6 APPLE SHAKE
7 VEGETABLE CLEAR SOUP

XII. Dieters' Menu

APPLE SHAKE PICTURE ON PAGE 133

A delicious breakfast drink.
Preparation time: a few minutes · No cooking · Makes 1 glass.

1 peeled and chopped apple
1 teacup cold skimmed milk
¼ teaspoon vanilla essence
1 drop *or* tablet saccharine
a pinch nutmeg *or* cinnamon

1. Blend the apple, milk, essence and saccharine in a liquidiser.
2. Sprinkle the nutmeg on top.

   ★ Serve immediately.

ORANGE AND APPLE DRINK

A filling breakfast juice.
Preparation time: a few minutes · No cooking · Makes 1 glass.

½ teacup fresh orange juice
¾ to 1 teacup peeled and
   chopped apple
a few pieces finely chopped
   apple and crushed ice to serve

1. Blend the apple and juice in a liquidiser.
2. Pour into a glass and add the apple pieces.
3. Top with crushed ice.

   ★ Serve immediately.

FACING PAGE
CHINESE BARBECUE

VITAMIN CUP PICTURE ON PAGE 133

A health drink.
Preparation time: a few minutes · No cooking · Makes 1 glass.

½ teacup chopped spinach
1 chopped carrot
1 tomato
a pinch salt
a pinch pepper
crushed ice and lemon slice to
    serve

1. Blend the spinach, carrot and tomato in a
   liquidiser.
2. Pour into a glass and add salt and pepper.

   ★ Top with crushed ice and serve with a slice of
   lemon.

WATER-MELON SORBET

A cold starter on warm days.
Preparation time: a few minutes · Setting time: 20 minutes · Serves 6.

2 teacups water-melon juice
1 teaspoon sugar
2 drops saccharine
1 packet (11 grams) strong
    gelatine
seedless grapes to serve

1. Mix the gelatine in ½ teacup of the
   water-melon juice and warm until the gelatine
   dissolves.
2. Add the rest of the juice and the sugar and
   saccharine.
3. Pour into ice-cube trays and put to set in the
   freezer compartment of a refrigerator.
4. When set, cut into pieces.

   ★ Serve chilled with grapes.

Variation: WATER-MELON ICE PICTURE ON PAGE 133 Omit the gelatine and freeze
the sweetened water-melon juice to make ice. You can serve this ice as a starter or
after the meal.

VEGETABLE CLEAR SOUP PICTURE ON PAGE 133

Light, quick and tasty.
Preparation time: a few minutes · Cooking time: a few minutes · Serves 6 to 8.

2 lettuce leaves
2 spinach leaves
1 sliced carrot
2 chopped spring onions
a few sliced mushrooms
½ teacup sliced cauliflower
1 teaspoon soya sauce
¼ teaspoon Ajinomoto powder
3 teaspoons oil
salt to taste
chillies in vinegar and soya
   sauce to serve

1. Tear the lettuce and spinach leaves into big pieces.
2. Heat the oil, add the carrot, spring onions, mushrooms, cauliflower and Ajinomoto powder and cook for 2 to 3 minutes.
3. Add the leaves and toss for a few seconds.
4. Add 7 teacups of very hot water.
5. Finally add the soya sauce and salt.

★ Serve immediately with chillies in vinegar and soya sauce.

HEARTY VEGETABLE SOUP

A filling soup.
Preparation time: 20 minutes · Cooking time: 25 minutes · Serves 6 to 8.

For the stock
2 onions
2 tomatoes
2 carrots
250 grams (9 oz.) white
   pumpkin
250 grams (9 oz.) cabbage
5 to 6 french beans

For the topping
1 chopped onion
½ teacup chopped cabbage
1 finely chopped carrot
1 large finely chopped tomato
2 tablespoons tomato ketchup
1 small can (225 grams) baked
   beans (optional)
1 teaspoon butter
salt and pepper to taste
chopped parsley to serve

For the stock
Cut the vegetables into big pieces, add 5 teacups of water and cook. When soft, prepare the stock by passing through a sieve.

How to proceed
1. Heat the butter and fry the onion for 1 minute.
2. Add the cabbage and carrots and cook for 2 minutes.
3. Add to the stock and boil for 10 minutes.
4. Add the tomato, tomato ketchup, baked beans, salt and pepper.

★ Sprinkle chopped parsley on top and serve hot.

GREEN SOUP

Inexpensive yet tasty.
Preparation time: 15 minutes · Cooking time: 30 minutes · Serves 6.

3 to 4 teacups fresh green peas
   pods
2 onions
2 spring onions
1 small head lettuce
1 teaspoon plain flour
2½ teacups skimmed milk
salt and pepper to taste

1. Clean the green peas pods.
2. Cut the onions, spring onions and lettuce into big pieces.
3. Mix the green peas pods and vegetable pieces and add 5 teacups of water. Cook in a pressure cooker.
4. When cooked, blend the mixture in a liquidiser. Strain.
5. Mix the plain flour and milk and add to the soup.
6. Add the salt and pepper and mix well.

★ Serve hot.

LEAFY VEGETABLE SOUP

Healthy and nutritious.
Preparation time: 15 minutes · Cooking time: 20 minutes · Serves 6.

1 bundle spinach
1 head lettuce
3 spring onions
2 onions
3 teacups skimmed milk
1 teaspoon plain flour
salt and pepper to taste

1. Chop the leafy vegetables and cut the onions into big pieces. Add 2 teacups of water and cook.
2. When cooked, blend in a liquidiser.
3. Mix the milk and plain flour. Add to the vegetable liquid.
4. Cook for about 5 minutes.
5. Add salt and pepper.

★ Serve hot.

GAZPACHO

A dieters' version of the classic cold soup.
Preparation time: a few minutes · No cooking · Serves 4.

4 chopped tomatoes
2 teacups tomato juice
4 teaspoons lemon juice
4 teaspoons vinegar
8 tablespoons finely chopped
  onions
1 clove crushed garlic
2 chopped cucumbers
4 finely chopped green onions
salt to taste

1. Blend the tomato, tomato juice, lemon juice, vinegar, onion and garlic in a liquidiser.
2. Add half the cucumber and blend again.
3. Taste and add salt.
4. Chill.

★ Serve chilled in individual cups, topped with green onions and the remaining cucumber.

PERFECTION SALAD

Vegetables in lemon jelly make a refreshing salad.
Preparation time: 20 minutes · Setting time: 20 minutes · Serves 6 to 8.

2 packets (11 grams each)
  strong gelatine
2 tablespoons lemon juice
2 tablespoons powdered sugar
3 drops saccharine
½ teaspoon salt
1 teacup sliced cabbage
½ teacup grated carrots
1 chopped capsicum
3 to 4 sticks celery (chopped)
lettuce leaves and grated carrots
  for decoration

1. Keep the vegetables in ice-cold water for 10 minutes. Drain.
2. Mix the gelatine, lemon juice, sugar, saccharine, salt and 600 ml. (20 fl. oz.) of water. Heat on a slow flame until the gelatine dissolves.
3. Pour the mixture into a flat dish, cool and set partially in the refrigerator.
4. When the mixture is partially set, break it up. Add the vegetables. Add sugar and salt if required.
5. Pour into a mould and put to set in the refrigerator.
6. Just before serving, dip the mould in hot water for a few seconds, loosen the sides and unmould on a plate.
7. Surround with lettuce leaves and grated carrots.

★ Serve cold.

FRUIT AND VEGETABLE SALAD PICTURE ON PAGE 133

Colourful and tasty.
Preparation time: 25 minutes · No cooking · Serves 6.

2 teacups shredded cabbage
1 sliced capsicum
2 grated carrots
1 teacup seedless grapes
segments of 2 oranges
½ teacup paneer (optional)
juice of ½ lemon
2 drops saccharine
salt to taste
Dieters' Thousand Island
   dressing, *page 141*, to serve

1. Keep the cabbage, capsicum and carrots in ice-cold water for 10 to 15 minutes.
2. Drain and place on a serving plate. Sprinkle the lemon juice, saccharine and salt and mix well. Add the fruit and paneer.

★ Serve with Dieters' Thousand Island dressing.

CUCUMBER AND MOONG DAL SALAD

A simple Indian salad.
Preparation time: a few minutes · No cooking · Serves 4 to 6.

3 chopped cucumbers
1 teacup moong dal
2 tablespoons chopped
   coriander
2 chopped green chillies
juice of 1 lemon
a few drops saccharine
salt to taste
grated coconut and fresh
   coriander for decoration

1. Soak the moong dal for 2 hours in warm water. Drain.
2. Mix all the ingredients. Store in the refrigerator.
3. When serving, sprinkle grated coconut and fresh coriander on top.

★ Serve cold.

140

BEAN SALAD

A protein-rich salad.
Preparation time: a few minutes · Cooking time: 15 minutes · Serves 6.

1 teacup rajma
1 teacup bean sprouts (optional)
1 teacup chopped spring onions
2 chopped tomatoes
1 tablespoon chopped parsley
½ teaspoon chilli *or* curry
　powder
salt to taste
lettuce leaves and radish
　for decoration

1. Soak the rajma overnight.
2. Next day, cook in a pressure cooker with a little water. Drain.
3. Add the bean sprouts, spring onions, tomatoes, chilli powder and salt and mix well.
4. Chill thoroughly.
5. Decorate with lettuce leaves and radishes.

★ Serve cold.

DIETERS' THOUSAND ISLAND DRESSING

PICTURE ON PAGE 133

Serve this tasty dressing with any fruit or vegetable salad.
Preparation time: a few minutes · No cooking · Makes 1¼ teacups.

1 teacup fresh curds made from
　skimmed milk *or* yoghurt
2 tablespoons skimmed milk
1 tablespoon tomato ketchup
a few drops chilli sauce
1 teaspoon chopped onion
½ teaspoon chopped capsicum
¼ teaspoon chopped green
　chillies
½ teaspoon mustard powder
1 drop saccharine
salt to taste

1. Tie the curds in a cloth and hang for 2 hours to allow the water to drain out.
2. Add the remaining ingredients and mix well.
3. Chill and store in the refrigerator.

DAHI BHURTA

A cool salad.
Preparation time: 10 minutes · Cooking time: 20 minutes · Serves 4 to 6.

1 large *or* 2 small eggplants (about 500 grams)
2 teacups fresh curds made from skimmed milk
2 chopped green chillies (optional)
salt to taste
chopped coriander for decoration

1. Grill or burn the eggplant on the gas until soft. Peel, wash and mash.
2. Add the curds, green chillies and salt.
3. Put in the refrigerator.
4. Just before serving, sprinkle coriander on top.

★ Serve cold.

SPROUTED MASALA MATH

A spicy sprouted curry.
Preparation time: 20 minutes · Cooking time: 20 minutes · Serves 6 to 8.

500 grams (1⅛ lb.) sprouted math
4 large tomatoes
salt to taste
chopped tomato, cucumber and onion to serve

For the paste
1 sliced onion
4 teaspoons khus-khus
3 sticks cinnamon
3 cloves
3 to 4 peppercorns
2 teaspoons coriander seeds
5 cloves garlic
8 to 10 Kashmiri chillies
1 teaspoon oil

1. Heat the oil and fry all the ingredients for the paste except garlic. Cook for 2 to 3 minutes on a medium slow flame. Add the garlic and make a paste.
2. Cut the tomato into big pieces, add ½ teacup of water and cook. When cooked, take out soup by passing through a sieve.
3. Mix the math, paste and 2 to 3 tablespoons of water and cook in a pressure cooker.
4. When cooked, add the tomato soup and salt.
5. Cook again for a few minutes.

★ Sprinkle chopped tomatoes, cucumber and onion on top and serve hot.

Note: If you like, you can use mixed sprouted lentils instead of math.

VALVAL

A South Indian dish cooked in coconut milk.
Preparation time: 20 minutes · Cooking time: 25 minutes · Serves 6 to 8.

100 grams (4 oz.) white
    pumpkin
100 grams (4 oz.) red pumpkin
100 grams (4 oz.) ridge gourd
100 grams (4 oz.) green peas
4 to 5 french beans
1 carrot
1 large fresh coconut
3 to 4 slit green chillies
3 to 4 curry leaves
¾ teaspoon cumin seeds
1 tablespoon plain flour
1 teaspoon ghee
1 drop saccharine *or* 1 teaspoon
    sugar
salt to taste

1. Slice the pumpkin, ridge gourd, french beans and carrot very thinly.
2. Grate the coconut, add 2 teacups of water and allow to stand for a little while. Blend in a liquidiser, strain and take out a thick milk. Add 2 teacups of water to the same coconut and allow to stand for a little while. Blend in a liquidiser, strain and take out thin milk.
3. Mix the thick coconut milk and the plain flour very well.
4. Heat the ghee and fry the cumin seeds for a few seconds. Add the chillies and curry leaves and fry again for a few seconds.
5. Add the vegetables, thin milk and salt and cook.
6. When the vegetables are soft, add the thick coconut milk, saccharine and salt. Cook for a few minutes.

    ★ Serve hot with chapatis.

BAIGAN BHURTA

A traditional Indian dish.
Preparation time: 10 minutes · Cooking time: 20 minutes · Serves 4 to 6.

1 large *or* 2 small eggplants
    (about 500 grams)
3 chopped spring onions
2 chopped tomatoes
1 teaspoon dhana-jira powder
1 teaspoon chilli powder
salt to taste
chopped coriander for
    decoration

1. Grill or burn the eggplant on the gas until soft. Peel, wash and mash.
2. Mix the onions, tomatoes and 2 teaspoons of water and cook for 2 to 3 minutes.
3. Add the eggplant, dhana-jira powder, chilli powder and salt and cook for a few minutes.

    ★ Sprinkle coriander on top and serve hot.

BAKED PANEER WITH VEGETABLES

PICTURE ON PAGE 133

Attractive and healthy.
Preparation time: a few minutes · Cooking time: 15 minutes · Serves 6.

2 teacups chopped paneer
2 teacups mixed boiled
   vegetables (cauliflower,
   carrots, french beans)
2 tablespoons fresh curds
salt to taste

To be ground into a paste
1 teacup chopped coriander
4 to 5 green chillies
2 tablespoons grated coconut
1 teaspoon salt
1 teaspoon sugar
juice of 1 lemon

1. Mix the paneer and vegetables.
2. Mix the paste with the curds.
3. Mix the vegetables and the paste. If you like, sprinkle a little milk over the vegetables to make the mixture moist. Add very little salt.
4. Wrap in aluminium foil and bake in a hot oven at 450°F for 10 to 15 minutes.

★ Serve hot.

MOONG DAL AND SPINACH

An enjoyable accompaniment.
Preparation time: 10 minutes · Cooking time: 20 minutes · Serves 4.

1 teacup moong dal
1 teacup chopped spinach
1 chopped onion
1 chopped green chilli
¼ teaspoon turmeric powder
1 chopped tomato
½ teaspoon chilli powder
1 teaspoon amchur powder
salt to taste
roasted cumin seed powder and
   chopped coriander to serve

1. Wash the moong dal.
2. Add the onion, green chilli, turmeric powder and 1½ teacups of water and boil.
3. When the dal is three-quarter cooked, add the remaining ingredients and cook for a few minutes more.
4. Sprinkle roasted cumin seed powder and chopped coriander on top.

★ Serve hot.

BAKED EGGPLANT IN TOMATO SAUCE

You will not believe that this tasty dish is so low in calories.
Preparation time: 10 minutes · Cooking time: 30 minutes · Serves 4 to 6.

2 medium eggplants
  (long variety)
1 to 2 teaspoons oil
salt to taste

For the tomato sauce

1 kg. (2¼ lb.) tomatoes
3 cloves crushed garlic
2 onions
½ teaspoon chilli powder
1 teaspoon oregano *or*
  ¼ teaspoon ajwain (optional)
salt to taste

For baking

3 tablespoons crumbled cottage
  cheese

1. Slice the eggplants.
2. Heat the oil in a non-stick frying pan and
   spread the eggplant slices over the hot oil.
3. Sprinkle a little salt, cover and cook until the
   eggplants are soft.

For the tomato sauce

1. Chop the tomatoes and onions.
2. Mix the tomatoes, onions and garlic.
   Cover and cook until soft.
3. Blend the mixture in a liquidiser.
4. Add the chilli powder, oregano and salt and
   cook for a few minutes.
5. Taste and if sour, add a drop of saccharine.

How to proceed

1. In a greased baking dish, make layers of
   eggplant and tomato sauce.
2. Cover with cottage cheese and bake in a hot
   oven at 450°F for 5 to 10 minutes.

   ★ Serve hot.

BAKED SAMOSAS

A tasty snack for dieters.
Preparation time: 20 minutes · Cooking time: 20 minutes · Serves 4.

For the dough
1 teacup whole meal flour
a pinch salt

For the filling
2 teacups finely chopped
  cabbage
2 chopped onions
1 teaspoon chilli-ginger paste
juice of 1 lemon
1 drop saccharine
2 tablespoons chopped
  coriander
salt to taste

For the dough
1. Mix the flour and salt and add enough water to make a soft dough.
2. Knead well.
3. Roll out very thin chapatis.
4. Cook on a tava for a few seconds.

For the filling
1. Sprinkle salt over the cabbage and leave for 10 minutes. Squeeze out the water.
2. Add the remaining ingredients and mix well.

How to proceed
1. Divide each chapati into two parts.
2. Make a cone from each part and fill with the stuffing mixture. Close each cone using a clove.
3. Toast the samosas on both sides in an oven toaster.

★ Serve hot with green chutney.

MOONG DAL SNACK

A breakfast snack.
Preparation time: 15 minutes · Cooking time: a few minutes · Serves 4 to 6.

1 teacup moong dal
3 chopped green chillies
2 tablespoons chopped
  fenugreek leaves (methi bhaji)
  or 1 tablespoon chopped
  coriander
a pinch asafoetida
¼ teaspoon soda bi-carb
salt to taste

1. Soak the dal for 2 to 3 hours. Drain.
2. Add the green chillies and 2 tablespoons of water and blend in a liquidiser.
3. Add the fenugreek leaves, asafoetida, soda bi-carb and salt.
4. Pour a little mixture at a time in a non-stick sandwich toaster or in a waffle iron. Cook for a few minutes. Alternatively, spread the mixture in a thali and steam.

★ Serve hot with green chutney.

CREAM CRACKER SNACK

A satisfying snack.
Preparation time: 20 minutes · Cooking time: 20 minutes · Serves 6.

For the cauliflower paste
1 teacup finely chopped
   cauliflower
1 teacup skimmed milk
1 chopped green chilli
salt to taste

For the spinach mixture
3 teacups chopped spinach
1 chopped green chilli
a pinch soda bi-carb
1 tablespoon water
salt to taste

For the snack
a few cream cracker biscuits
cottage cheese

For the cauliflower paste
1. Mix the cauliflower and milk and cook on a
   slow flame.
2. Add the green chilli and salt and mash well.

For the spinach mixture
Mix all the ingredients and boil until the
spinach is cooked. Drain and keep aside.

How to proceed
1. On each cream cracker biscuit, spread a little
   cauliflower paste and then a little spinach
   mixture.
2. Sprinkle a little cottage cheese on top.
3. Warm the biscuits for about 10 minutes.

   ★ Serve hot.

Variation: You can also use tomato sauce, *page 145,* in place of the spinach mixture.

ORANGE AND STRAWBERRY PUDDING

You can make this pudding using any seasonal fruit combination with orange juice.
Preparation time: 15 minutes · Setting time: 20 minutes · Serves 6 to 8.

segments of 2 oranges
1 teacup sliced strawberries
2 sliced bananas
1 packet (11 grams) strong gelatine
350 ml. (12 fl. oz.) orange juice
2 tablespoons orange squash
1 to 2 drops saccharine
a few drops red colouring

1. Mix the gelatine in 4 tablespoons of water and warm on a slow flame until it dissolves.
2. Add the gelatine mixture to the orange juice. Add the orange squash and saccharine. Pour into a mould and set the mixture partially in the refrigerator.
3. When the mixture is set partially, break it up, add the fruit and colouring, mix well and put to set again in the refrigerator.
4. Just before serving, dip the mould in hot water for a few seconds, loosen the sides and unmould on a plate.

★ Serve cold.

BAKED APPLE

Simple and sweet.
Preparation time: 20 minutes · Cooking time: 30 minutes · Serves 4.

4 medium dessert apples
4 teaspoons seedless raisins
a little cinnamon powder
a little powdered sugar

1. Core the apples with a pointed knife or corer.
2. Scrape off the skin from the top portions (about 12 mm.) of each apple and make a few light vertical slits in the upper portions (so that the skin does not burst during cooking).
3. Sprinkle a little cinnamon and sugar into the core cavities and add the raisins.
4. Place the apples in a baking dish. Add water so that the bottom quarter portion of the apples is covered.
5. Bake in a moderate oven at 350°F for 30 minutes or until the apples are tender.

★ Serve hot.

XIII. Tabletop Cookery

CHINESE BARBECUE PICTURE ON PAGE 134

Cook this dish in small portions for a few people at a time.
Make a complete meal with soup.
Preparation time: 30 minutes · Cooking time: a few minutes per batch.

sliced onions
chopped green onions
shredded cabbage
sliced capsicums
sliced tomatoes
grated carrots
bean sprouts
boiled noodles
Ajinomoto powder
soya sauce
ginger water
chilli oil
chilli garlic paste
chillies in vinegar
oil
salt to taste
garlic bread to serve

Advance preparation
For the ginger water
 Grate 50 mm. (2") piece of ginger, add 1 teacup
 of water and keep aside for ½ hour.

For the chilli oil
 Break 15 to 20 red chillies into big pieces. Heat
 1 teacup of oil and add the chillies. Switch off
 the gas and cover. Strain after 2 hours.

For the chilli garlic paste
 Grind 10 to 12 garlic cloves with 10 red chillies
 and ½ teacup of water.

For the chillies in vinegar
 Cut 6 to 7 green chillies and add to 1 teacup of
 white vinegar.

Table cooking
 Heat 2 to 3 tablespoons of oil at a time on a
 large pau-bhaji tava on a high flame. Add a few
 onions and vegetable pieces and a few pinches
 of Ajinomoto powder and stir for a while. Add
 a little ginger water, chilli oil, chilli garlic paste,
 chillies in vinegar, soya sauce and salt, one at a
 time. Finally add a few noodles and stir.

 ★ Serve hot with hot garlic bread. Repeat with
 the remaining ingredients.

 Note: You can add ingredients in proportions
 of your choice.

QUICK GREEN PEA SNACK

Try this delightful snack when peas are fresh and tender.
Preparation time: 15 to 20 minutes · Cooking time: a few minutes · Serves 4 to 6.

For the fried noodles

1 teacup plain flour
½ teaspoon salt
2 teaspoons oil
oil for deep frying

Other ingredients

3 teacups green peas
2 chopped onions
¼ teaspoon Ajinomoto powder
3 to 4 chopped green chillies
½ teaspoon chilli powder
½ tablespoon chopped
   coriander
2 chopped tomatoes
1 teaspoon soya sauce
   (optional)
1 teacup fried bread croutons
4 tablespoons oil

Advance preparation
For the fried noodles

1. Sieve the flour with the salt.
2. Add the oil and mix well.
3. Add enough water to make a soft dough.
4. Divide the dough into 3 parts.
5. Roll out with the help of a little flour as thinly as possible.
6. Cut into long thin strips with a sharp knife.
7. Deep fry in hot oil.

Table cooking

1. Heat the oil in a large griddle or flat vessel and fry the onions for 1 minute.
2. Add the green peas and Ajinomoto powder and cook for 3 to 4 minutes.
3. Add the green chillies, chilli powder and coriander.
4. After 2 minutes, add the tomatoes, soya sauce, croutons and noodles. Cook for a little while.

   ★ Serve hot.

FACING PAGE
VEGETABLE SIZZLERS

MUSHROOMS AND NOODLES

Connoisseurs' choice.
Preparation time: 10 minutes · Cooking time: a few minutes · Serves 4.

1 can (450 grams) button
   mushrooms
1 teacup boiled noodles
1 finely chopped onion
1 clove crushed garlic (optional)
1 teaspoon caraway seeds
¾ teacup white wine
1 teacup thin cream
2 to 3 tablespoons grated
   cheese
3 tablespoons butter
salt and pepper to taste
chopped parsley for decoration

Advance preparation
1. Slice the mushrooms. Keep aside the liquid
   from the can if wine is not being used.
2. Add 1 tablespoon of butter and a pinch of salt
   to the noodles and cook for 1 minute.

Table cooking
1. Heat 2 tablespoons of butter in a large frying
   pan, add the onion, garlic and caraway seeds
   and fry for 1 minute.
2. Add the mushrooms and fry again for
   2 minutes.
3. Add the wine (or liquid from the mushrooms),
   cream, salt and pepper and half of the cheese.
4. Make a border with the noodles or simply add
   and mix, according to preference.
5. Sprinkle the remaining cheese on top and cook
   for 1 minute.

★ Decorate with chopped parsley and serve
hot.

FACING PAGE
1 FRUIT FLAMBÉ AND ICE-CREAM
2 SNAKE COFFEE

VEGETABLE SIZZLERS PICTURE ON PAGE 151

A grand meal by itself, well worth the time and effort.
Preparation time: 1½ hours · Cooking time: a few minutes · Serves 8 to 12.

For the vegetable cutlets
3 potatoes
3 carrots
250 grams (9 oz.) french beans
500 grams (1⅛ lb.) cabbage
2 to 3 onions
¼ teaspoon turmeric powder
1 teaspoon chilli powder
3 tablespoons plain flour
2 tablespoons chopped
    coriander
2 to 3 chopped green chillies
2 tablespoons ghee
salt to taste
bread crumbs
ghee *or* refined oil for frying

For the stuffed capsicums
5 to 6 capsicums
ingredients for vegetable cutlets
    excluding bread crumbs and
    ghee for frying

For the stuffed tomatoes
5 to 6 medium sized tomatoes
1 teacup cooked rice
4 to 5 tablespoons tomato
    ketchup
2 to 3 teaspoons plain flour
¼ teaspoon chilli powder
salt to taste

Advance preparation

For the vegetable cutlets
1. Chop all the vegetables finely.
2. Heat the ghee in a vessel and fry the onions for
    1 minute. Add the turmeric and chilli powders
    and salt and continue cooking until the
    vegetables are cooked.
3. Sprinkle the plain flour on the vegetables, mix
    and cook again for a few minutes.
4. Mash the vegetables. Add the coriander and
    green chillies and mix well.
5. Shape into cutlets.
6. Roll in bread crumbs and shallow fry in ghee.

For the stuffed capsicums
1. Remove the top part of the capsicums and
    scoop out the centres.
2. Proceed to make the stuffing as per steps 1 to 4
    for vegetable cutlets.

For the stuffed tomatoes
1. Remove the top portion of the tomatoes and
    scoop out the centres.
2. Mix the rice, tomato ketchup, flour, chilli
    powder and salt.
3. Fill the tomatoes with this mixture.

Table cooking
1. Heat a large flat griddle or tava.
2. Pour a little tomato ketchup in the centre. Add
    the stuffed capsicums and tomatoes and cook
    for 2 minutes. When cooked, push on the sides
    to make an outer border.
3. Put a little butter in the centre. Add the green
    peas and carrots, sprinkle salt and pepper on
    top and cook for 1 minute. When cooked, push
    on the sides to make a second border.

Other ingredients

boiled green peas
boiled carrots
fried potato chips
boiled spaghetti
cloves crushed garlic (optional)
grated cheese (optional)
tomato ketchup
butter
salt and pepper
warm crisp bread to serve

4. Pour a little tomato ketchup in the centre. Add the potato chips, sprinkle salt and pepper on top and cook for 1 minute. When cooked, push on the sides to make yet another border.
5. Finally, put a little butter in the centre. If you like, add crushed garlic and fry for a few seconds. Add the spaghetti, sprinkle salt on top and cook for a few minutes.
6. Put the cutlets in between the tomatoes and capsicums. If you like, sprinkle cheese all over.
7. Let your guests help themselves (or serve in individual plates) directly from the griddle. Provide at least for 1 cutlet, 1 capsicum and 1 tomato per guest.

★ Serve hot with warm, crisp bread.

POTATO RÖSTI

The popular Swiss dish!
Preparation time: a few minutes · Cooking time: 20 minutes · Serves 6.

1 kg. (2¼ lb.) potatoes
140 grams (5 oz.) grated cheese (use combination of two cheeses)
1 finely chopped onion
1 finely chopped green chilli (optional)
2 tablespoons butter
salt and pepper to taste

Advance preparation
1. Wash the potatoes and put in boiling water for 7 minutes. Drain and cool.
2. Peel the potatoes. Grate coarsely or slice. Sprinkle salt and pepper on top.

Table cooking
1. Melt the butter in a large frying pan. Add the onion and cook for 1 minute.
2. Spread the potatoes in the pan.
3. Sprinkle the chilli and cheese on top and cook on a slow flame for 10 minutes.
4. Turn the potato mixture upside down in one piece.
5. Cook until crisp and brown on the underside.
6. Loosen around the edges with a knife.
7. Invert and take out in one piece.

★ Serve hot.

NOODLES WITH TOMATO AND CREAM SAUCES PICTURE ON PAGE 26

A delightful way of serving Italian pasta.
Preparation time: 1 hour · Cooking time: a few minutes for each batch · Serves 6 to 8.

For the white noodles
200 grams (7 oz.) plain flour
1 egg
2 teaspoons oil
½ teaspoon salt

For the green noodles
200 grams (7 oz.) plain flour
1 egg
2 teaspoons oil
½ teaspoon salt
1 teacup chopped spinach
¼ teaspoon lemon juice

For the tomato gravy
1 kg. (2¼ lb.) tomatoes
1 large finely chopped onion
1 large finely chopped carrot
2 sticks celery, finely chopped
3 tablespoons fresh cream
1 teaspoon chilli powder
1 teaspoon oregano *or* 2 pinches ajwain
2 teaspoons sugar
2 tablespoons refined *or* salad oil
salt to taste

For the cream sauce
2 teacups thin white sauce, *page 164*
100 grams (4 oz.) fresh cream
2 tablespoons grated cheese
salt and pepper to taste

To serve
grated cheese

Advance preparation
For the white noodles
1. Mix all the ingredients and add a little cold water to make a stiff dough.
2. Knead for 10 minutes until smooth and silky.
3. Roll out the dough until so thin that the table underneath can be just seen.
4. Make flat noodles with a noodle cutter or by cutting into thin strips with a knife.
5. Dry and store or dry for at least 3 to 4 hours before boiling.

For the green noodles
1. Put the spinach, lemon juice and 1 tablespoon of cold water in a liquidiser and blend.
2. Mix the flour, egg, oil and salt. Add enough spinach liquid to make a stiff dough.
3. Knead for 10 minutes until smooth and silky.
4. Roll out the dough very thinly.
5. Make flat noodles with a noodle cutter or by cutting into thin strips with a knife.
6. Dry and store or dry for at least 3 to 4 hours before boiling.

For the tomato gravy
1. Put the tomatoes in hot water. After 10 minutes, remove the skin and grate into a pulp.
2. Heat the oil and fry the onion, carrot and celery for at least 5 minutes.
3. Add ½ teacup of water and cook for 3 to 4 minutes.
4. Add the tomato pulp, chilli powder, oregano, sugar and salt.
5. Boil on a slow flame for at least 30 minutes.
6. Add the cream and mix.

For the cream sauce
Mix all the ingredients

Table cooking
1. Boil plenty of water in a large vessel. Add 2 tablespoons of oil and 1 teaspoon of salt. Put a few white noodles at a time as required and cook until soft.
2. In another large vessel, boil plenty of water and add 2 tablespoons of oil and 1 teaspoon of salt. Put a few green noodles at a time as required and cook until soft.
3. Remove a few cooked white noodles with a wire sieve, allow the water to drain out.

★ Serve with individual sauces on a plate. Repeat with the green noodles.

Note: You can also use ready-made white and green noodles instead of making them yourself.

PANEER KABABS

A popular vegetable grill, quick and easy to prepare.
Preparation time: 10 minutes · Cooking time: a few minutes · Makes 2 skewers.

400 grams (14 oz.) paneer
2 large tomatoes
2 large capsicums
2 cucumbers
4 tablespoons tomato ketchup
mint chutney to serve

To be made into a marinating mixture
1½ teacups fresh curds
2 teaspoons grated onions
2 pinches coarsely powdered ajwain
25 mm. (1") piece ginger, grated
¼ teaspoon salt

Advance preparation
1. Cut the paneer, tomatoes, capsicums and cucumbers into pieces suitable for putting on skewers.
2. Dip the paneer pieces in the tomato ketchup. Remove and keep in the marinating mixture for 1½ hours.
3. Marinate the tomato, capsicum and cucumber pieces in the mixture for 1½ hours.

Table cooking
Put the marinated paneer, capsicum, tomato and cucumber pieces one by one on skewers. Roast on a gas fire or in an oven for about 10 minutes, rotating the skewers from time to time.

★ Serve hot with mint chutney.

SIZZLING VEGETABLES

A simpler and quicker version of vegetable sizzlers.
Preparation time: 30 minutes · Cooking time: a few minutes · Serves 6 to 8.

100 grams (4 oz.) butter
a few boiled potato halves
a few boiled cabbage quarters
2 to 3 teacups mixed boiled
    vegetables (french beans,
    carrots, green peas)
1 teacup boiled spaghetti
4 to 5 teaspoons chilli sauce
¾ teacup tomato ketchup
6 cloves crushed garlic
1 chopped onion
4 to 5 tablespoons grated cheese
salt to taste

Table cooking

1. Heat the butter in a large skillet and fry the garlic and onion for 2 to 3 minutes.
2. Put the potatoes and the cabbage on the sides of the skillet.
3. Place the remaining boiled vegetables in the centre.
4. Top with spaghetti and sprinkle the chilli sauce, tomato ketchup, cheese and salt. Mix well. Go on stirring for a few minutes.

★ Serve hot.

SAUTÉED EGGPLANT

A very delicately spiced dish for the eggplant lovers.
Preparation time: a few minutes · Cooking time: 10 minutes · Serves 4 to 6.

1 large or 2 medium eggplants
    (about 500 grams)
1 teacup thin cream
2 teaspoons lemon juice or
    2 tablespoons fresh curds
¾ teacup sliced mushrooms
    (optional)
2 cloves crushed garlic
½ teaspoon chilli powder
½ teaspoon pepper powder
1 tablespoon chopped parsley
2 tablespoons butter
salt to taste

Advance preparation

1. Slice the eggplants. Sprinkle with salt and leave for 20 minutes. Rinse and drain.
2. Mix the cream with the lemon juice. If using curds, beat the cream and the curds. Add the sliced mushrooms.

Table cooking

1. Heat the butter in a frying pan and fry the garlic for 1 minute.
2. Spread the eggplant slices on the pan and cook each side for 2 to 3 minutes.
3. Add the cream and mushroom mixture.
4. Sprinkle the parsley, chilli and pepper powders and salt and cook for 1 minute. If you like, sprinkle a little lemon juice also.

★ Serve hot.

MUSHROOM AND ONION FONDUE PICTURE ON PAGE 25

For the mushroom lovers.
Preparation time: a few minutes · Cooking time: a few minutes · Makes about 3 teacups.

1 can (450 grams) mushrooms
1 small onion
1 clove garlic
200 grams (7 oz.) cheese, made up of equal quantities of two different types of cheeses
1 teacup milk
2 level tablespoons plain flour
1 tablespoon butter
salt and pepper to taste
bread pieces to serve

Advance preparation
1. Drain and chop the mushrooms. Keep aside the liquid from the can.
2. Chop the onion.
3. Crush the garlic.

Table cooking
1. Heat the butter and fry the mushrooms and onion for 1 minute.
2. Add the garlic and fry again for a few seconds.
3. Add the flour and fry again for 1 minute.
4. Add the milk, liquid from the can and the two types of cheeses and cook until the mixture becomes thick.
5. Add salt and pepper, mix well and pour into a fondue pot. If you like, sprinkle a little chilli powder on top.

★ Serve hot. Let your guests serve themselves by dipping bread pieces into the hot fondue.

Note: This mixture can also be spread on toast pieces and served as mushrooms on toast.

SWISS FONDUE

The traditional fondue.
Preparation time: a few minutes · Cooking time: a few minutes · Makes 2 teacups.

2 teacups white wine
2 heaped teacups grated cheese (use combination of two cheeses)
1/8 teaspoon nutmeg powder
1 teaspoon cornflour
salt to taste
bread pieces to serve

Table cooking
1. Warm the wine in a chafing dish.
2. Add the cheese and cook until it melts.
3. Mix the cornflour in a little water and add to the cheese.
4. Add the nutmeg powder and very little salt and cook for a little while.

★ Let your guests dip the bread pieces into the hot cheese mixture using forks or skewers.

CHOCOLATE FONDUE PICTURE ON PAGE 82

This sinfully rich dessert will recall the childhood pleasure of fingers dipped in chocolate.
Preparation time: 10 minutes · Cooking time: 10 minutes · Serves 6 to 8.

100 grams (4 oz.) plain *or* milk
   chocolate, broken into small
   pieces
1 tablespoon plain flour
½ teacup milk
3 teaspoons cocoa (approx.)
200 grams (7 oz.) beaten cream
4 to 5 tablespoons sugar
½ teaspoon vanilla essence
1 tablespoon butter
2 tablespoons brandy (optional)
stewed or fresh fruit,
   marshmallows, cake pieces
   for dipping

Table cooking

1. Melt the butter and fry the flour on a slow flame for ½ minute.
2. Add the milk, chocolate pieces, cocoa, cream, sugar and 1 teacup of water. Go on stirring and cooking on a slow flame until the mixture becomes thick.
3. Put the mixture in a chafing dish. Stir in the vanilla essence and brandy.

★ Let your guests serve themselves by dipping fruit, marshmallow or cake pieces in the hot mixture.

Note: Adjust the quantity of cocoa according to its strength.

PINEAPPLE FLAMBÉ

A simple but rich dessert.
Preparation time: a few minutes · Cooking time: 10 to 15 minutes · Serves 3 to 4.

6 pineapple slices (from can)
2 tablespoons honey
2 tablespoons orange juice
2 tablespoons brandy
6 cherries (from can)
1 tablespoon butter
whipped cream *or* vanilla
   ice-cream to serve

Table cooking

1. Heat the butter in a large frying pan.
2. Arrange the pineapple slices in the pan, put one cherry in the centre of each slice and cook for 5 to 10 minutes.
3. Add the honey and orange juice and cook for 3 minutes.
4. Warm the brandy in a large spoon, set alight and pour the burning brandy over the fruit.

★ Serve with whipped cream or vanilla ice-cream.

FRUIT FLAMBÉ AND ICE-CREAM PICTURE ON PAGE 152

A rich fruit flambé which can be eaten by itself or with ice-cream.
Preparation time: a few minutes · Cooking time: a few minutes · Serves 6 to 8.

4 teacups mixed fruits (mixture of canned *or* fresh fruits)
1 small can (450 grams) orange juice
2 tablespoons sugar
1 teaspoon butter
2 tablespoons Cointreau
2 tablespoons brandy
vanilla ice-cream to serve

Advance preparation
Drain the fruit.

Table cooking
1. Melt the sugar in a large saucepan.
2. Add the butter while the sugar is melting.
3. Add the orange juice and boil for a few minutes.
4. Add the fruit and boil again for 1 minute.
5. Add the Cointreau.
6. Warm the brandy in a large spoon, set alight and pour over the fruit.

★ Serve hot with vanilla ice-cream.

BANANA FLAMBÉ

When short of time, make this simple and quick dessert.
Preparation time: a few minutes · Cooking time: a few minutes · Serves 4 to 6.

4 bananas
juice of 1 orange
50 grams (2 oz.) brown sugar
1 tablespoon butter
1 teaspoon grated orange rind
3 tablespoons brandy
sweetened cream to serve

Table cooking
1. Cut the bananas lengthwise and place in a frying pan cut side down.
2. Add the orange juice, sugar, butter and orange rind and cook gently for a few minutes, turning the bananas frequently.
3. Warm the brandy in a large spoon, set alight and pour the burning brandy over the bananas.

★ Serve at once with sweetened cream.

BRANDIED APPLES

Brandied apples and vanilla ice-cream make a perfect match.
Preparation time: a few minutes · Cooking time: 10 minutes · Serves 8.

8 medium-sized dessert apples
1 teacup white wine
100 grams (4 oz.) sugar
juice of 1 orange
juice of ½ lemon
2 tablespoons butter
4 tablespoons brandy
vanilla ice-cream to serve

Advance preparation
1. Peel the apples.
2. Mix the white wine, sugar and 1 teacup of water in a vessel and heat.
3. When it starts boiling, add the orange and lemon juices.
   Add the apples and cook gently till tender.

Table cooking
1. Pour the syrup in which the apples have been cooked into a chafing dish.
2. Arrange the apples carefully in the syrup.
3. Add the butter and cook for a few minutes.
4. Warm the brandy in a large spoon or ladle, set alight and pour the burning brandy over the apples.

   ★ Serve at once with vanilla ice-cream.

BRANDIED ORANGES

Oranges with a different flavour.
Preparation time: a few minutes · Cooking time: a few minutes · Serves 2 to 3.

3 peeled and sliced oranges *or* orange segments
2 tablespoons icing sugar
4 tablespoons thick cream
2 teaspoons powdered sugar
1 tablespoon brandy
2 tablespoons butter

Table cooking
1. Heat the butter in a frying pan, add the oranges and cook for 2 to 3 minutes.
2. Sprinkle the icing sugar on top.
3. Beat the cream, sugar and brandy and serve on top of the oranges.

   ★ Serve hot.

SNAKE COFFEE PICTURE ON PAGE 152

A fitting finale to a glorious dinner.
Preparation time: 10 minutes · Cooking time: a few minutes · Makes 4 to 5 small glasses.

2 to 3 tablespoons granulated sugar
2 tablespoons whisky
3 to 4 tablespoons white rum
3 to 4 teaspoons brown sugar
3 level teaspoons coffee
1 sweet lime
6 tablespoons fresh cream

Table cooking

1. Melt the sugar in a frying pan. When it becomes brown in colour, roll the rims of the glasses in the caramelised sugar. The sugar will harden on the glass rims in a minute or two.
2. In another frying pan, put the brown sugar and whisky and warm. Set the whisky alight and allow to burn for a while.
3. Prepare the coffee in about 2½ teacups of water. Add this coffee to the burning whisky.
4. Cut the peel of the sweet lime in a spiral so that it gives a serpentlike shape. Discard the sweet lime.
5. Warm the lime peel in a spoon.
6. Warm the white rum in a large spoon. Set alight.
7. Hold the peel with any prong type arrangement over the coffee and with the other hand, pour the white rum gradually over the peel so that the lighted rum flows down the peel whilst burning and finally drops into the coffee.
8. Dip the peel into the coffee and remove.

★ Pour the coffee into the prepared glasses, top with cream and serve immediately.

XIV. Basic Recipes

WHITE SAUCE

Preparation time: a few minutes · Cooking time: a few minutes · Makes 2 teacups.

2 tablespoons butter
2 tablespoons plain flour
2 teacups milk
salt and pepper to taste

1. Melt the butter, add the flour and cook for 2 minutes without browning, while stirring throughout.
2. Remove from the heat and gradually add the milk. Mix until well blended.
3. Return to heat and cook slowly, stirring throughout until the sauce thickens. Add salt and pepper and mix well.

Note: This is a thick coating sauce used for cauliflower, cheese, filling flans, baked casserole dishes etc.
For thin pouring sauce, use 1 tablespoon of butter and 1 tablespoon of flour with 2 teacups of milk.

Variation: Add 4 to 5 tablespoons of grated cheese and a little made mustard, if you like, to 2 teacups of white sauce. Mix well.

SALAD CREAM

Preparation time: a few minutes · No cooking · Makes about 1¼ teacups.

225 grams (8 oz.) fresh cream
5 to 6 tablespoons salad oil *or* refined oil
1 teaspoon mustard powder
3 teaspoons powdered sugar
½ teaspoon salt
3 teaspoons lemon juice
¼ teaspoon pepper

Mix all the ingredients together.
Store in a refrigerator.

THOUSAND ISLAND DRESSING PICTURE ON PAGE 35

Preparation time: a few minutes · No cooking · Makes about 1½ teacups.

1 teacup mayonnaise *or*
1 teacup salad cream, *page 164*
1 tablespoon tomato ketchup
1 teaspoon chilli sauce
1 tablespoon chopped
capsicum
1 tablespoon finely chopped
onion
½ teaspoon salt
1 tablespoon chopped
hard-boiled egg (optional)
a few finely chopped pieces of
gherkin, olives and pimento
(optional)

Mix all the ingredients together.
Store in a refrigerator.

SHORTCRUST PASTRY

Preparation time: 10 minutes · Cooking time: given under individual recipes.

225 grams (8 oz.) plain flour
115 grams (4 oz.) cold
margarine *or* butter
a good pinch salt

1. Sieve the flour and salt together.
2. Cut the margarine with a knife. Rub into the flour with finger tips.
3. Gradually add enough ice-cold water (approx. 2 to 3 tablespoons) to make the dough into a rolling consistency.
4. Lightly flour the rolling pin and the pastry board.
5. Roll the pastry to required thickness and shape, lifting and turning to keep it light.
6. As a general rule, pastry should be baked in a hot oven at 450°F, but exact baking times and temperatures are given in individual recipes.

SPONGE CAKE FOR PUDDINGS

Preparation time: 15 minutes · Cooking time: 25 minutes.

For large cake
3 large eggs
85 grams (3 oz.) self-raising flour (*or* plain flour can be used adding ¾ teaspoon baking powder)
115 grams (4 oz.) sugar
4 tablespoons melted butter *or* margarine

For small cake
2 large eggs
55 grams (2 oz.) self-raising flour (*or* plain flour can be used adding ½ teaspoon baking powder)
85 grams (3 oz.) sugar
3 tablespoons melted butter *or* margarine

1. Sieve the flour.
2. Grease and dust a baking tin. Use approx. 250 mm. × 125 mm. (10" × 5") or 175 mm. (7") diameter tin for the large cake; and 225 mm. × 100 mm. (9" × 4") or 150 mm. (6") diameter tin for the small cake.
3. Beat the eggs and sugar very well until thick and double in quantity.
4. Fold in the well-sieved flour carefully and gently with a metal spoon.
5. Fold in 2 tablespoons of hot water (1½ tablespoons for the small cake) and the butter.
6. Pour the mixture into the prepared baking tin.
7. Bake in a hot oven at 400°F for 15 minutes.
8. The cake is ready when it leaves the sides of the tin and is springy to touch.
9. Take out from the oven and leave for 1 minute. Invert the tin over a rack and tap sharply to remove.

Variation: CHOCOLATE SPONGE CAKE Proceed as for sponge cake for puddings but reduce the self-raising flour quantity by 15 grams (½ oz.) and instead use 15 grams (½ oz.) cocoa.

PRALINE POWDER

Preparation time: 10 minutes · Cooking time: 10 minutes · Makes about 1 teacup.

¾ teacup almonds *or* cashewnuts
¾ to 1 teacup sugar

1. Melt the sugar in a heavy saucepan, add the nuts and cook on a slow flame until rich brown in colour.
2. Spread the mixture on a tin.
3. When cold, powder coarsely.
4. Store in an air-tight jar.

EGGLESS CHOCOLATE SPONGE CAKE

Preparation time: 10 minutes · Cooking time: 30 minutes.

½ can (of a 400 grams full can) condensed milk
1 level teaspoon baking powder
½ teaspoon soda bi-carb
125 grams (4½ oz.) self-raising flour
1 tablespoon cocoa
1 tablespoon chocolate powder
60 ml. (2 fl. oz.) melted butter *or* margarine
1 teaspoon vanilla essence

1. Sieve the flour, cocoa, chocolate powder, baking powder and soda bi-carb together.
2. Mix the condensed milk, flour, 75 ml. (2½ fl. oz.) water, vanilla essence and melted butter thoroughly.
3. Grease and dust a 150 or 175 mm. (6" or 7") diameter tin.
4. Pour the cake mixture into the prepared tin.
5. Bake in a hot oven at 400°F for 10 minutes. Thereafter, reduce the temperature to 350°F and bake for a further 15 minutes.
6. Cool the cake.

BUTTER ICING

Basic butter icing
Cream 55 grams (2 oz.) soft butter (or margarine) until soft and white. Do not warm. Work in 85 grams (3 oz.) sieved icing sugar with flavouring and colouring as required. To make a firmer icing, use 115 grams (4 oz.) of icing sugar.

Chocolate butter icing
Add about ¾ tablespoon of chocolate powder, 1 teaspoon cocoa and a few drops of vanilla essence to the basic butter icing.

Coffee butter icing
Work in ½ teaspoon of coffee essence (or 1 teaspoon soluble powder dissolved in 2 teaspoons water) in the basic butter icing. Do this gradually; otherwise the mixture will curdle.

Vanilla butter icing
Add ½ teaspoon vanilla essence to the basic butter icing.

FATLESS SPONGE CAKE

Preparation time: 15 minutes · Cooking time: 25 minutes.

For large cake
3 large eggs
85 grams (3 oz.) plain flour
85 to 115 grams (3 to 4 oz.) fine
   tea sugar

For small cake
2 large eggs
55 grams (2 oz.) plain flour
55 to 85 grams (2 to 3 oz.) fine
   tea sugar

1. Sieve the flour.
2. Grease and dust a baking tin. Use approx. 250 mm. × 125 mm. (10" × 5") or 175 mm. (7") diameter tin for the large cake, and 225 mm. × 100 mm. (9" × 4") or 150 mm. (6") diameter tin for the small cake.
3. Beat the eggs and sugar very well until thick and double in quantity.
4. Fold in the well-sieved flour carefully and mix gently with a metal spoon.
5. Pour the mixture into the prepared baking tin.
6. Bake in a hot oven at 400°F for 15 minutes.
7. The cake is ready when it leaves the sides of the tin and is springy to touch.
8. Take out from the oven and leave for 1 minute. Loosen the sides with a knife, invert the tin over a rack and tap sharply to remove.

Variation: FATLESS CHOCOLATE SPONGE CAKE Proceed as above adding 1 level tablespoon of cocoa to the flour at step 1.

EGGLESS SPONGE CAKE

Preparation time: 10 minutes · Cooking time: 20 minutes.

½ can (of a 400 grams full can) condensed milk
140 grams (5 oz.) self-raising flour
60 ml. (2 fl. oz.) melted butter *or* margarine
1 level teaspoon baking powder
½ teaspoon soda bi-carb
1 teaspoon vanilla essence

1. Sieve the flour, baking powder and soda bi-carb together.
2. Mix all the ingredients together, add 75 ml. (2½ fl. oz.) water and beat well.
3. Grease and dust a 150 mm. (6") diameter tin.
4. Pour the mixture into the prepared tin.
5. Put to bake in a hot oven at 400°F for 10 minutes. Thereafter, reduce the temperature to 300°F and bake for a further 10 minutes.
6. Cool the cake.